MANAGING OUR WASTE 2021

View from the Global South

**Practical
ACTION**

Practical Action Publishing Ltd
27a Albert Street, Rugby, CV21 2SG, UK
www.practicalactionpublishing.org

A catalogue record for this book is available from the British Library.
A catalogue record for this book has been requested from the Library of Congress.

ISBN 978-1-78853-095-8 Paperback
ISBN 978-1-78853-098-9 Ebook

Citation:
Practical Action (2021) *Managing Our Waste 2021: View from the Global South*,
Practical Action Publishing, Rugby <https://doi.org/10.3362/9781788530989>.

Since 1974, Practical Action Publishing has published and disseminated books and
information in support of international development work throughout the world.
Practical Action Publishing is a trading name of Practical Action Publishing Ltd
(Company Reg. No. 1159018), the wholly owned publishing company of
Practical Action. Practical Action Publishing trades only in support of its
parent charity objectives and any profits are covenanted back to Practical Action
(Charity Reg. No. 247257, Group VAT Registration No. 880 9924 76).

Practical
ACTION
PUBLISHING

CONTENTS

FOREWORD

HRH The Prince of Wales

We live on a planet with finite resources. If we are all to enjoy a sustainable future, we must use those resources wisely. We urgently need greater investment in circular economies where materials are recovered, re-used and recycled. At the same time, poor waste management is causing enormous environmental damage, destroying the delicate balance of land and marine ecosystems and emitting greenhouse gases. For people who live with the consequences of uncollected waste, the problems are severe for their health, welfare and economic wellbeing. As with many global problems, the impacts of unsustainable waste management of all kinds are felt most acutely by some of the world's poorest people – those living in urban slums and low-income settlements.

I have been well aware of, and deeply frustrated by, these issues for many years. The Terra Carta action plan I launched to support the Sustainable Markets Initiative aims to accelerate significantly the transition to systems where sustainability is mainstreamed. The future of waste, as a previously unrealized resource, is key to this, with the potential to deliver transformational results on a global scale for Nature, People and Planet. The opportunities for positive solutions are enormous, particularly if we recognize what already exists. Small enterprises and informal workers across towns and cities in the emerging market countries of the Commonwealth, and beyond, are already recovering and recycling waste in large volumes. In Africa especially, young people are leading the way, and with the right kinds of support and market incentives, they could be empowered for better lives and livelihoods through green businesses.

As Practical Action's Patron, I greatly value their commitment to finding solutions that really work to help people in poverty change their world. This report illustrates Practical Action's focus on people-centred approaches, based on an in-depth understanding of what is happening on the ground. It shows how the actions that will create lasting and equitable change are those with people at their heart, and which seek to improve the lives of the poorest while working more sustainably within the finite resources of the one planet we all share.

I warmly welcome this *Managing our Waste 2021* report, and can only encourage readers to follow its lead in putting people at the heart of a rapid transition to a more sustainable future of waste utilization.

PRAISE FOR MANAGING OUR WASTE

Waste is one of the biggest challenges of the urban world and it is at the core of human and sustainable development. The origins of municipal waste management systems at the turn of the 20th century – undoubtedly an important development prompted by concerns with public health – brought about a technocratic approach to waste, which ultimately lacked connections with dimensions related to a broader concept of human development. It is time we put people front and centre in waste management. It is possible to couple environmental and social concerns in the design of urban systems. Practical Action's Managing Our Waste 2021 report 'brings people back to the heart of the narrative'. With a good mix of benchmark indicators, qualitative and participatory methods, the report explores physical and governance elements of waste management in the selected cities, and takes a deep dive into livelihoods aspects, including the gendered dimensions of waste management.

Sonia Maria Dias
Waste specialist, Women in Informal Employment: Globalizing and Organizing (WIEGO)

In this analysis, Practical Action has used state of the art assessment tools, including the WasteAware Benchmark Indicators. Their work in testing and evolving the idea of a waste services ladder is also a highly valuable contribution. We should be putting people's experiences and the overall improvement of people's lives first – considering both short and long-term implications. Our assessments need to ensure they are achieving this, and that is something central to this report.

Dr Costas Velis
Lecturer in Resource Efficiency Systems, School of Civil Engineering, Leeds University

Solid waste management is the 'Cinderella' among the essential utility services. Despite the crisis of some 40 per cent of the world's population having no access, it has received very limited attention from either international agencies or mainstream development charities. I have been supporting Practical Action for nearly 50 years, so I warmly welcome this important new report which fills that gap. Most development work tackles the issue from the 'top down', and often focuses on (large scale) infrastructure. Much of my work over the last 25 years has focused on expanding performance assessment and planning of SWM systems in developing countries to include governance (including stakeholder inclusivity) alongside technical aspects; and to consider the often 'informal' recycling sector alongside 'formal' municipal waste management. Practical Action has taken that one step further, to strengthen the 'bottom-up', people-centred aspects. Sustainable waste and resource management needs to work for the poorest people, providing both a quality service which keeps slum areas clean and healthy, and a decent livelihood for the multitude of workers who deliver collection and recycling services. Both the revised assessment methods, the four insightful case studies and the four priority themes work well. I commend to you this important new manifesto to put people back at the centre of how we manage our solid wastes.

Professor David C. Wilson
Visiting Professor in Resource and Waste Management, Imperial College London; Lead author of UNEP's Global Waste Management Outlook

ABOUT PRACTICAL ACTION

We are an innovative international development group, putting ingenious ideas to work so people in poverty can change their world. Our vision is for a world that works better for everyone. We help people find solutions to some of the world's toughest problems, challenges made worse by catastrophic climate change and persistent gender inequality.

We were founded over 50 years ago by radical economist E.F. Schumacher, who challenged the conventional aid thinking of the day. He believed in solutions suited to context, equipping people with the skills and knowledge to change their situation, economic systems that work for all, and living within the planet's means. While development approaches have changed, these founding beliefs still drive us, and have more widely come of age.

Today, we remain deeply rooted in the reality of people living in poverty. We start small, to understand what's already working and how improvements can be made. We develop innovative, community-powered, and locally owned solutions that achieve transformative change in lives and livelihoods. But we aim 'big' – focusing on what will deliver the systems change required and the best role we can play.

And we seek bold collaborations to work at scale. We are a trusted partner for communities, governments and international organizations, and, increasingly, the private sector.

ACKNOWLEDGEMENTS

Managing Our Waste 2021: View from the Global South is produced by Practical Action. It was compiled by a core team comprising Dr Lucy Stevens, Caspar Way, and Noemie de La Brosse (Oxford Policy Management), with contributions from Mike Webster (Systemiq). The report is envisaged as the first in an ongoing series highlighting key issues in solid waste management from a people-centred perspective. We set out to ensure the report is rich in grounded information from the people at the frontline of the problems and their solutions. We intentionally set out to mainstream gender issues and give space to the voices of women as waste-service users and service providers.

Our first thanks, therefore, go to the women and men in Satkhira, Dhenkanal, Kisumu, and Dakar who participated in the *Managing Our Waste* research, offering valuable insights into the waste management problems they face, their coping strategies, and the contribution they make as entrepreneurs and service providers.

This report would not have been possible without the Practical Action teams in Bangladesh, India, Kenya, and Senegal, and the consultants whose commitment and careful work provided the information on which this report draws. For their contributions, we thank Uttam Kumar Saha, Mehrab Ul Goni, and Fariduzzaman Shapon (Practical Action Bangladesh), with Monir Chowdhury and his team from Commitment Consultants in Bangladesh; Birupakshya Dixit (Practical Action India), with Ranjan Mallick and his team from GeoSpatial Solutions in India; Mathew Okello (Practical Action East Africa), with Harrison Kwach, and Joshua Okello and his team from QDATAMS in Kenya; and Cheikh Ahmadou Mbodji (Practical Action Consulting West Africa), with Daniel Vidal and his team in Senegal. Special thanks also to Nicola Greene (OPERO Services) and her team for helping to craft a coherent fieldwork pack and delivering training to all four country teams.

Recognition is also due to our peer reviewers whose insights and feedback were highly valuable in shaping the final report, in particular to Mansoor Ali (consultant) and David C. Wilson (consultant). Thanks also go to Mercer Design for producing the infographics and accompanying poster, and to the Practical Action Publishing team for their flexibility and professionalism throughout. To the talented photographers who provided us with wonderful photographs to use in the report, thank you. We hope these images will help readers to visualize the diverse stories of waste management and the struggles faced, but also the skills and expertise that exist across the world. Finally, thank you to all those individuals and organizations who shared information from their work and allowed their data and references to be used for *Managing Our Waste 2021*.

ABBREVIATIONS AND ACRONYMS

3R	reduce, reuse, recycle
ANSD	Agence Nationale de la Statistique et de la Démographie (Senegal)
APHRC	African Population and Health Research Centre
CBO	community-based organization
CIWM	The Chartered Institution of Wastes Management
GIZ	Deutsche Gesellschaft für Internationale Zusammenarbeit
GoB	Government of Bangladesh
HDI	Hasiru Dala Innovation
IIED	International Institute for Environment and Development
ILO	International Labour Office
ISWA	International Solid Waste Association
KIWAN	Kisumu Waste Management Association
KKPKP	Kagad Kach Patra Kashtakari Panchayat union
KNBS	Kenya National Bureau of Statistics
MCC/MRF	micro-composting centre / material recovery facility
MEFP	Ministere de L'Economie, des Finances et du Plan (Senegal)
MoEF	Ministry of Environment and Forests, Bangladesh
MoEF	Ministry of Environment and Forestry, Kenya
MoENR	Ministry of Environment and Natural Resources, Kenya
MoEFCC	Ministry of the Environment, Forestry and Climate Change (India)
MSW	municipal solid waste
NAMA	Nationally Appropriate Mitigation Action
NEMA	National Environment Management Authority (Kenya)
PET	polyethylene terephthalate
PFC	Plastics for Change
PPE	personal protective equipment
PROMGEDE	Projet de promotion de la gestion intégrée et de l'économie des déchets solides (Senegal)
PPP	public–private partnership
PVC	polyvinyl chloride
SWaCH	worker-owned cooperative of waste pickers in Pune, India
SWM	solid waste management
tCO_2e	tonnes of carbon dioxide equivalent
UCG	Unité de Coordination de la Gestion des déchets solides (national coordinating unit, Senegal)
UNEP	United Nations Environment Programme
UNICEF	United Nations Children's Fund
WASH	water, sanitation, and hygiene
WHO	World Health Organization
WIEGO	Women in Informal Employment, Globalizing and Organizing
WRA	Water Resources Authority (Jamaica)
WRI	World Resources Institute

PHOTO CAPTIONS AND CREDITS

Front cover. S.K. Haider, informal waste picker and collector in Dhenkanal, Odisha State, India. (Credit: Shreeyanka Chowdhury)

Executive summary. Gabriel Obuo, an informal waste worker (right), collecting household waste from Pamela Akinyi (left), a resident of Nyalenda, Kisumu, Kenya. (Credit: Mwangi Kirubi)

Introduction. Municipal waste dump site and waste worker in Satkhira, Bangladesh. (Credit: Md. Sakib Nawaz)

Page 3. Arouna Fofana, informal waste picker and collector in Dakar, Senegal. (Credit: Bineta Nasr)

Approaches to solid waste management. Hazrat, municipal and informal waste worker in Satkhira, Bangladesh. (Credit: Md. Sakib Nawaz)

Page 7. Waste dumpsite in Dakar, Senegal. (Credit: Bineta Nasr)

People-centred assessment. S.K. Haider, an informal waste worker, collecting sorted waste from a household in Dhenkanal, Odisha State, India. (Credit: Shreeyanka Chowdhury)

Satkhira, Bangladesh. Abu Saleh, municipal and informal waste worker in Satkhira, Bangladesh. (Credit: Md. Sakib Nawaz)

Page 30. Municipal waste workers clearing waste from communal disposal point in Satkhira, Bangladesh. (Credit: Md. Sakib Nawaz)

Dhenkanal, Odisha, India. Sasmita Sarkar, municipal waste worker in Dhenkanal, Odisha State, India. (Credit: Shreeyanka Chowdhury)

Kisumu, Kenya. Gabriel Obuo, an informal waste worker, and his collecting cart in Nyalenda, Kisumu. (Credit: Mwangi Kirubi)

Dakar, Senegal. Babacar Ndiaye, informal waste picker and collector in Dakar, Senegal. (Credit: Bineta Nasr)

People-centred waste services. Waste service user emptying separated waste into a municipal waste collection service for recycling in Dhenkanal, Odisha State, India. (Credit: Shreeyanka Chowdhury)

Page 70. Municipal waste workers clearing streets as a team in Satkhira, Bangladesh. (Credit: Md. Sakib Nawaz)

Page 72. Plastic waste is shredded and processed at a municipal recycling plant in Dhenkanal, Odisha State, India. (Credit: Shreeyanka Chowdhury)

Conclusion. Lucy Atieno Oudo, resident and informal waste service user in Nyalenda, Kisumu, Kenya. (Credit: Mwangi Kirubi)

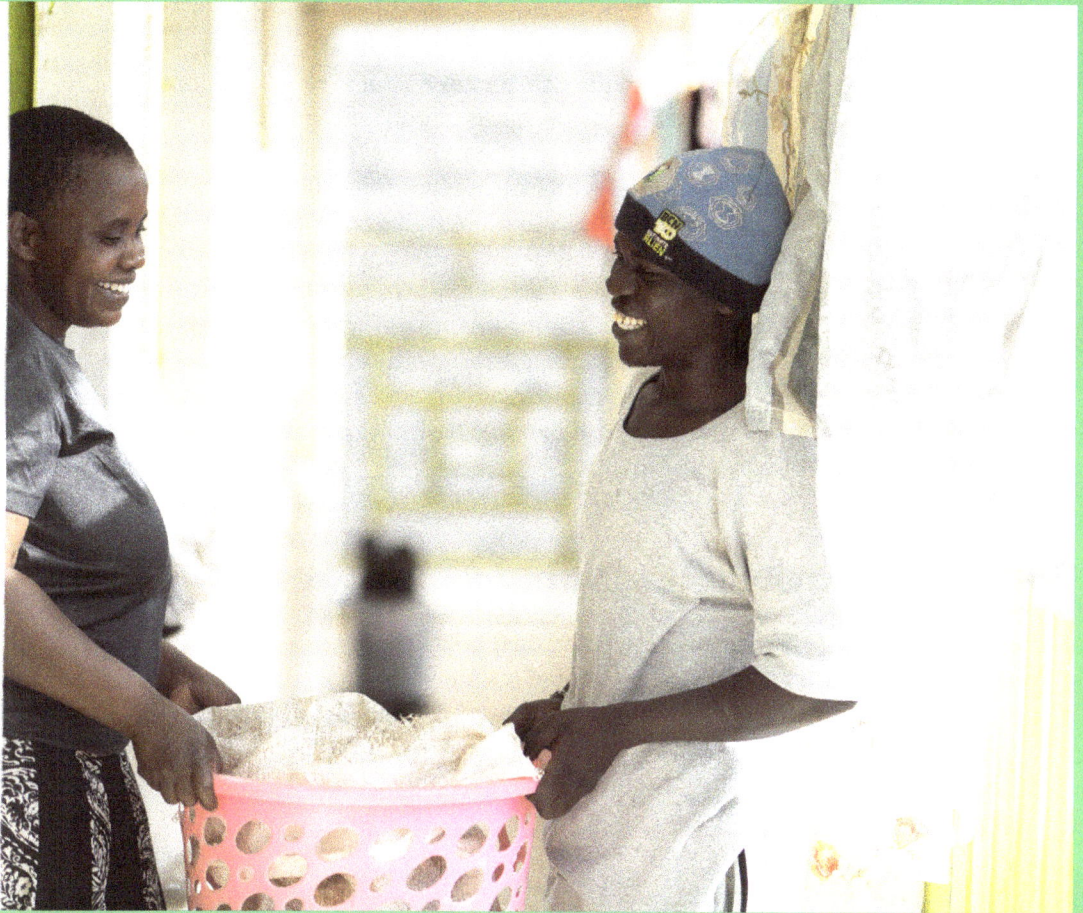

EXECUTIVE SUMMARY

There are already 4.35 billion people living in urban areas globally, and every day this population generates solid waste that needs to be safely disposed. However, 2 billion people live without any form of waste collection, and over 90 per cent of waste in low-income countries is openly dumped or burned. As patterns of consumption change, volumes of waste increase, and municipal solid waste generation in lower-income cities in Africa and Asia is predicted to double by 2030.

Far-reaching impacts of the waste crisis

The impacts of this waste crisis are far-reaching. Our focus is primarily on the people living in slum and low-income communities who are directly impacted by the rotting remains of uncollected waste; and informal sector workers whose working conditions put them at risk every day. In terms of health, uncollected waste provides a breeding ground for diseases and disease-carrying pests. When waste is openly burned, it can exacerbate acute respiratory infections. Waste can also block toilets and water drainage systems, causing spills of polluted water and sewage. Informal sector waste workers are at the frontline of health impacts and at risk of injury, infections, and disease. They also face social exclusion, harassment, and abuse.

As waste piles up, it can cause serious environmental damage. Heavy metals and other dangerous materials can leak, destroying valuable habitats and farmland. Poor communities that often live near large dumpsites are the most directly impacted. Plastics are having serious impacts on freshwater and marine ecosystems. Dumpsites produce 12 per cent of total global methane emissions. Burning of waste emits black carbon which, while short-lived, has a disproportionate warming effect, contributing between 2 and 10 per cent of climate change emissions. The economic costs also mount up, with damage to livelihoods, and costs from ill health and disasters like flooding.

A local priority but a global afterthought

Waste management is often an important local political and economic priority, absorbing on average 20 per cent of municipal budgets. Yet, despite its far-reaching impacts, it has a low priority on the global development agenda, attracting only 0.3 per cent of development aid in 2012. This has increased a little with funds targeting marine litter and circular economy. The inclusion of waste management in the Sustainable Development Goals in 2015 (target 11.6.1) was welcome. However, the sector remains weak compared with other basic services like water, sanitation, and hygiene.

Only 0.3% of development aid went to solid waste management in 2012

A people-centred approach grounded in global and local evidence

Analysis of solid waste management tends to focus on volumes, composition, and flows of waste, and on infrastructure and equipment needed to solve the problem. Recent environmental concerns have reinforced this. There is an urgent need to bring people back to the heart of the narrative: the impact they suffer and the potential they hold for more effective solutions. We suggest refocusing on systems that work for people in terms of quality of service, accessibility, affordability, better working conditions, and resource recovery, which bring more value to the poorest in waste value chains.

Our key message about a people-centred approach is grounded in four contrasting case study cities where fieldwork took place between October 2020 and February 2021. In Africa, these were Dakar, Senegal; and Kisumu, Kenya. In Asia, we selected two smaller towns: Satkhira in Bangladesh and Dhenkanal in Odisha State, India.

Findings also drew on existing best-practice tools such as the WasteAware benchmark indicators, and UN-Habitat's Waste Wise Cities Tool, adding additional qualitative and participatory methods to better understand the realities from the ground. We took care to explore gendered perspectives throughout.

To shift the focus from waste quantities to services, we adapted and refined the ladder of waste services as proposed by UN-Habitat. Measuring services in terms of four attributes – access, quality, impact of waste on the locality, and separation for recycling – we placed households on a five-step ladder from 'fully controlled' to 'no service'. Levels of service were compared

There is an urgent need to bring people back to the heart of the narrative

by gender and between wealth categories to reveal the depth of inequalities at the city level.

Key findings

In this study we put people back at the heart of the waste management picture. Our case studies illustrated a diverse set of contexts and existing provision of waste services. However, some common threads emerged.

Low access to even basic waste services

Citywide, the proportion of residents without a basic waste management service ranged between 61 and 93 per cent. This was greater in slum and low-income areas, with levels between 84 and 100 per cent of residents, except in Dhenkanal. Levels of access that are this low would not be acceptable for other forms of basic service.

Within households, impacts of poor waste management were experienced differently between men and women. In focus groups and interviews, women highlighted the tangible ways in which waste affects their lives and those of their children. They are also responsible for managing waste at household levels and sometimes (not always) for paying for services.

Men and women are impacted differently by poor waste management

Low focus on waste with the greatest impact

While a great deal of global attention focuses on plastics, the vast majority of waste by weight is organic. It is plentiful, heavy, messy, and polluting. When dumped indiscriminately, it harbours pests and diseases and significantly impacts the living environment. We only found a few examples of informal businesses collecting separated organic material.

Plastics make up a smaller proportion of household waste by weight, but are light, bulky, and long-lived in the environment. There are ready markets for dense plastics, which are widely collected by informal businesses, but this is not the case for thin plastics or composite materials and plastic sachets. In some places, this waste is burned but that carries its own health hazards. Other types of waste people found difficult to dispose of included single-use nappies and menstrual pads, which is a growing market.

Informal waste workers make recycling happen

In all cities, the largest proportion of recovery and recycling was handled by informal waste entrepreneurs. Between 20 and 84 per cent of households separate waste to give or sell to traders. These collectors, pickers, and aggregators are skilled in sorting, grading, cleaning, and processing waste to meet the needs of the recycling economy, and they also understand waste supply chains. However, they can be limited from expanding by stringent regulatory requirements, a lack of secure access to land, or finance to invest in equipment.

Almost all workers in informal waste businesses face forms of discrimination and abuse, and are at risk when dealing with hazardous waste without sufficient protective equipment or safe processes. Women are often in the minority among workers and can be confined to particular roles, meaning they can only access less valuable waste streams. We did find examples of associations that were actively working in three of the four cities to improve the lives of members.

Informal waste entrepreneurs handled the largest proportion of recovery and recycling in all cities

Improving collection services does not always support recycling

Local authorities often find it hard to secure sufficient resources to deliver their mandate effectively, especially in secondary towns. Realizing there is demand for waste collection services, municipalities have often licensed the private sector to improve collection rates. Municipal efforts to boost collection can sometimes in fact lead to lower rates of recycling, and local authorities rarely manage to engage with or harness the dynamism of businesses involved in recovery and recycling. We found the resources, capacity, and support available to municipal and city waste managers was extremely limited, although the example of Dhenkanal shows there is scope for ambitious change.

Municipal efforts to boost collection can sometimes lead to lower rates of recycling

A call for people-centred action

Around the world there are a number of promising examples of what can be achieved through a shift away from traditional approaches (Chapter 2). Our analysis suggests four areas of action for a more people-centred approach.

- **Monitoring waste management as a people-centred service**. Adopting a ladder of access to waste services and disaggregating by wealth and gender highlights where action is needed. Targets should be set based on this to improve the proportion with access to at least basic waste management services.
- **Tackling the waste that affects people the most**. Encouraging even more household source separation, supported by new options for waste streams that are the most polluting or hazardous for people, in particular women and children.
- **Improving the lives and working conditions of informal waste workers**. A first step is to recognize and value the contribution of informal waste collection, recycling, and trading businesses. Discrimination, abuse, and gender inequalities need to be addressed, and more value from waste should be secured for those in the informal sector. This requires new public–private partnerships and systems to create space for the expertise and dynamism in this sector.
- **Integrating the voice of those most affected**. At all levels, waste policies need to focus not only on environmental benefits but also on improving the lives of the poorest communities and workers. Their voices need to be heard in all key decision-making processes.

Making these changes requires action from a wide range of stakeholders, including city managers, national governments, global and national businesses, and development institutions and funders. Action on waste management cuts across a range of traditional development sectors from urban development, livelihoods and economic development, youth empowerment, and environmental movements. Opportunities are growing, and the time is now to ensure they are harnessed for the greatest possible benefit to the most vulnerable people and the planet.

1 INTRODUCTION

We are now an urban species. By 2050 almost seven in 10 people will live in towns and cities, many in mega-cities in the global South (UNDESA, 2018). Urbanization leads to increases in the volumes and complexity of the solid waste generated, and the amount of waste produced globally is projected to double by 2050 from 2017 levels (Kaza et al., 2018). This makes getting a grip on waste management ever more critical, especially as the areas of most rapid urbanization are also those without comprehensive waste collection.

Two billion people are living without waste collection and 3 billion without controlled waste disposal (UNEP/ISWA, 2016). Developing countries have lower waste collection coverage but spend on average 20 per cent of their municipal budgets on waste management, yet over 90 per cent of waste in low-income countries is still openly dumped or burned (Kaza et al., 2018).

Improper waste management has serious health and environmental consequences and, if not addressed, will undermine efforts to achieve the Sustainable Development Goals (SDGs) (Kaza et al., 2018). Poor management of solid waste leads to a range of negative impacts (CIWM/WasteAid, 2018) on:

- the environment – pollution of surface and ground water; climate-changing greenhouse gas emissions; air pollution; marine plastics; harm to wildlife; flooding;
- human health – respiratory diseases; childhood stunting; water-borne diseases; infectious diseases;

- the economy – healthcare costs; productivity losses; damage from flooding; reduced tourist income; clean-up costs; missed opportunities; social inequality.

Good waste management as a development opportunity

Waste can also be an economic opportunity, particularly for marginalized groups. Dumped laptops and smartphones are fixed in the back streets of Accra or Lagos, textiles recycled in the 'shoddy yards' of Panipat, India, and ships scrapped for reuseable materials on the beaches of Cox's Bazaar, Bangladesh. This is the inclusive secondary economy in action, and it employs millions of people worldwide.

The multiple links between improved solid waste management and the Sustainable Development Goals are outlined in Table 1.1. Managing waste properly can help deliver all the SDGs (Wilson, 2021).

Table 1.1 Waste and the Sustainable Development Goals

green = direct link
number = SDG target that explicitly requires a basic level of waste management
light green = direct link but difficult to measure
yellow = indirect link

	1. Access for all to basic waste collection services	2. Stopping uncontrolled dumping and open burning	3. Managing all waste properly, particularly hazardous waste	4. Reducing waste and creating recycling jobs	5. Halving food waste, and reducing food losses in the supply chain	6. Governance factors which underpin sustainable waste management
1. End poverty	1.4					
2. Zero hunger						
3. Good health and wellbeing						
4. Quality education						
5. Gender equality						
6. Clean water and sanitation		6.3				
7. Affordable and clean energy						
8. Decent work and economic growth						
9. Industry, innovation, and infrastructure						
10. Reduced inequalities						
11. Sustainable cities and communities	11.1, 11.6	11.6	11.6			
12. Responsible consumption and production			12.4	12.5	12.3	
13. Climate action						
14. Life below water	14.1	14.1				
15. Life on land						
16. Peace, justice, and strong institutions						
17. Partnerships for the goals						

Source: Wilson, 2021: Figure 7.1

Meanwhile, many municipal governments are moving towards formalizing waste collection systems. If this process is not well managed, there is a risk of making the situation worse: vulnerable people in the informal recycling sector might lose their livelihoods and, in some instances, formal systems have reduced collection coverage and recycling rates.

Solid waste – neglected in the global development agenda

In 2012, only 0.3 per cent of development aid went to solid waste management (Lerpiniere et al., 2014). So far, the focus has been on treatment and containment of materials, with less attention on finding financially sustainable solutions that ensure collection for all and don't harm the livelihoods of those already working with waste. A side-effect of this inattention is the poor quality of waste data, with few opportunities for sharing experiences between practitioners.

But there is increasing recognition that an inclusive circular economy can offer a triple win: a clean and healthy urban environment, jobs for the most vulnerable, and a way of addressing the climate emergency and marine litter.

Our objectives for this report

There is renewed interest in what actually works in a lower-income context. This publication aims to put people firmly at the centre of the issue, placing the quality of waste services (collection, transport, disposal, reuse, recycling) at its core, and looks at opportunities for the most marginalized people to be part of the solution. Rather than focusing solely on quantities and categories of waste, we focus on the systems that work for people in terms of the quality of service, accessibility, affordability, and working conditions. Ultimately, what matters is whether waste is collected or not, whether one can derive some value from some of it, and how it is managed once it is picked up. Our key research questions are:

- Why does good solid waste management matter for the poorest communities?
- How do the poorest manage their waste? What is the impact when there is no service?
- How can we set up inclusive systems using effective public–private partnerships that cover the chain from householders, waste pickers, aggregators, and re-processors, ensure value is evenly spread, and allow all participants to move themselves out of poverty?

We recognize the flexibility and the reach of the informal recycling sector. They offer services to those who are unable to afford or live in places unserved by the formal sector (Wilson et al., 2006; Velis, 2017). Indeed, perhaps informal approaches point to a future of high quality, comprehensive, and flexible collection systems that traditional municipal approaches sometimes struggle to deliver.

The scale of the global waste crisis is truly overwhelming, with one in four living without proper waste management. The evidence can be seen in oceans full of plastic, smouldering mega-dumps on the edge of most cities in developing countries, and thousands of communities simply overwhelmed with rubbish. Something clearly is not working as it should. It is time to look anew at the issue, focusing on approaches that mean that everyone can have their waste collected, and benefit from a clean and healthy environment.

2 APPROACHES TO SOLID WASTE MANAGEMENT

It could be argued that waste is simply the 'effluence of affluence'. As economies develop and populations grow, ever increasing volumes of waste are generated, and the composition diversifies from one dominated by organic waste, to include increased volumes of 'dry' packaging, such as paper, metals, glass, e-waste, and plastics.

Waste is by no means a new challenge for urban planners. For instance, 19th-century London witnessed a series of epidemics directly linked with poor sanitation and poor solid waste management. Over 250,000 people died from cholera between 1848 and 1854, and smallpox, typhoid, enteric fever, and typhus were also major killers (Herbert, 2007).

The way that waste and recycling collections are organized tends to evolve with the economic development of urban areas. Regulation strengthens and the capacity of the government to deliver and manage services increases (Wilson, 2007). Public health concerns lead to the organization of municipal collection and banning of open burning and dumping, followed by steps to improve waste disposal and containment in sanitary landfills. Ultimately, environmental issues direct policy, with a focus on segregating waste, producer responsibility, fiscal instruments, and behaviour change strategies. Whiteman et al. (2021) define nine 'development bands' based on how waste systems have been observed to evolve, summarized in Box 2.1.

Box 2.1 How do waste management systems develop?

These stages have been observed as the 'mainstream' approaches to developing waste collection and disposal systems:

Bands 1–4: Early phases of system development. In the first stage, most households receive no waste collection service and have to self-manage their waste. In bands 2 and 3, services are established and expanded but are still not reaching everyone. Some better standards start to apply to disposal. In band 4, control is consolidated and collection reaches more difficult-to-service areas.

Band 5: The target baseline. At this stage, at least 95 per cent of waste is collected with controlled disposal, meeting SDG indicator 11.6.1.

Bands 6–9: Greater quality and controls. In these development bands two distinct approaches are taken. One focuses on market-oriented systems where the priority is to keep costs relatively low and the balance between disposal and recycling is dictated by market forces (bands 6 and 7). A second approach is one which sets regulations to prioritize high rates of recovery. In bands 8 and 9 either fiscal instruments (taxes, recycling credits, etc.) or rules and obligations are used to drive up recycling rates.

Band Zero. This is the aspirational end-point of a truly circular, 'zero waste' economy, which has not yet been achieved by any city or country.

Source: Whiteman et al. (2021)

The process outlined in Box 2.1 requires financial resourcing and strong central government. As urbanization progresses, the question for development practitioners is whether a degrading urban environment for the poorest is simply something that must be accepted. Is it necessary to wait until the quality of governance and public finance is strong enough to collect and contain solid waste, and does this inevitably mean pushing aside the informal sector to make way for public or private collectors? Or are there alternative approaches that can avoid these negative impacts and produce the same or better outcomes with lower costs?

Why does decent waste management for all matter?

Poor solid waste management has serious health, environmental, and economic consequences and addressing these issues is key to achieving the Sustainable Development Goals (Kaza et al., 2018).

Health impacts

Proximity to open dumps has been linked with the upsurge and spread of pathogenic infections, including cholera and other diseases, in various African cities (Osei and Duker, 2008; Abul, 2010; Suleman et al., 2015; Jerie, 2016).

Uncollected waste has a direct impact on the efficacy of toilet and water drainage systems by blocking, filling, and reducing the efficiency of these systems, creating a breeding ground for vectors associated with faecal-oral transmission. UN-Habitat data shows rates of diarrhoea are twice as high where solid waste is not collected (UN-Habitat, 2009), and children who grow up in such insanitary surroundings are prone to environmental enteropathy (Korpe et al., 2012; Ali et al., 2016), a condition of chronic intestinal inflammation. This results in chronic malnutrition (ibid.), stunting (Prendergast and Kelly, 2012), impeded neurocognitive development (Bhutta and Guerrant, 2017; John et al., 2017), and reduced efficacy of oral vaccination (Czerkinsky and Holmgren, 2015; Gilmartin and Petri, 2015).

Uncollected waste is often openly burned. The rate of acute respiratory infections is six times higher for children living in households where solid waste is burned in the yard (Scheinberg et al., 2010). Recent estimates show that uncontrolled burning of household waste causes an extra 270,000 premature deaths every year globally (Kodros et al., 2016), with suggestions that emissions of many air pollutants are significantly under-estimated because open waste burning is not included (Wiedenmyer et al., 2014).

Acute respiratory infections in children are six times higher in households burning waste

Even where waste is collected, there is often no proper disposal site. It is estimated that 40 per cent of the world's waste is disposed of at uncontrolled dumpsites (UNEP/ISWA, 2015). Children and adolescents living and going to school near the Dandora mega-dumpsite in Nairobi, Kenya, reported upper respiratory tract infections, chronic bronchitis, asthma, fungal infections, and allergic and unspecified dermatitis. Blood samples from children in the vicinity of Dandora showed that half of the children examined had blood lead levels equal to or exceeding internationally accepted toxic levels of 10 µg/dl (Kimani, 2005). There is often no monitoring at these sites or any environmental engineering to prevent escape of waste into the surrounding land and watercourses (ISWA, 2016). Infiltration of leachate from uncontrolled sites is a particular threat in small island states, such as Jamaica, where around one-quarter of groundwater is contaminated (WRA, 2008).

For those living at dumpsites, who pick through the waste, there are constant threats of injury, vermin, disease, and death. In March 2017, 113 people died when a dumpsite at Addis Ababa in Ethiopia collapsed (Duggan, 2017). A month later, an informal dump in Colombo City in Sri Lanka collapsed, killing 28 and leaving hundreds of families homeless (Kotelawala, 2017).

Economic impacts

In some areas, up to a third of cattle and half of goats swallowed enough plastic to make them prone to disease, emaciated, or low slaughter weight (Tiruneh and Yeswork, 2010; Mushonga et al., 2015); fish stocks can be reduced or polluted due to solid waste leaking into oceans; drains blocked by waste, notably plastics, can cause flooding that destroys property, as is the case with annual floods in East and West African, and Indian, cities (Scheinberg et al., 2010), and income from tourism can be majorly blighted by poor waste management.

In value-for-money terms, the costs to society of inaction exceed the financial costs of proper waste management by a factor of 5–10 (UNEP/ISWA, 2015). A recent study found that community-based waste management offers US$10 in benefits for every $1 invested, also reducing the need for more expensive, centralized waste management facilities by up to 90 per cent (Gower and Schroeder, 2018).

Waste and climate change

There are several links between climate change and waste: methane from dumpsites represents 12 per cent of total global methane emissions, the second largest contributor in 2010 (Hoornweg and Bhada-Tata, 2012). Methane contributes around 17 per cent of the total radiative forcing from all greenhouse gases (Stocker, 2013). The 1.6 billion tonnes of carbon dioxide–equivalent emissions associated with global solid waste management estimated for 2016 are anticipated to increase to 2.6 billion tonnes by 2050 (Kaza et al., 2018).

Meanwhile, recent research suggests that black carbon (soot) emissions from open burning of waste has a climate impact equivalent to 2–10 per cent of global CO_2Eq emissions, 2–8 times larger than the emissions arising from the decomposition of equivalent amounts of biodegradable waste. Black carbon has a global warming potential up to 5,000 times greater than carbon dioxide (CO_2), alongside other localized detrimental health impacts (Reyna-Bensusan et al., 2019).

The carbon impact of the production and disposal of single use plastics is also significant. In 2019, the production and incineration of plastic was

Methane from dumpsites represents 12% of total global methane emissions

estimated to have added more than 850 million metric tonnes of greenhouse gases to the atmosphere. This estimate does not account for 32 per cent of plastic packaging waste that is known to remain unmanaged, for open burning of plastic, for incineration that occurs without any energy recovery, or for other practices that are difficult to quantify (Kistler and Muffett, 2019).

On the positive side, a global shift to a circular economy, including greater reuse, longevity of materials, and use of recycled feedstock would tackle 45 per cent of global carbon emissions (Ellen MacArthur Foundation, 2019). Beyond that, the emissions associated with ever increasing levels of consumption are currently responsible for up to 60 per cent of global greenhouse gas emissions and between 50 and 80 per cent of total land, material, and water use (Ivanova et al., 2015).

So how do the poorest have their waste managed?

The urban poor receive little to no formal waste collection, while richer areas are far better served

It has been widely noted that in many cases the urban poor receive little to no formal waste collection. For instance, whilst around 50 per cent of households in non-slum areas have access to waste collection services in Benin, only around 10 per cent in slum areas receive collections. Around 60 per cent of waste is collected in non-slum areas in Ethiopia, whereas around 30 per cent in slum areas receive a collection (UN-Habitat, 2009).

Why does this happen? In many cases, the lack of waste collection is due to an inability to pay for formalized private sector collections and/or a physical inability for formalized waste collectors to reach inaccessible informal communities (Godfrey, 2018). One common scenario is when contractors are given sole rights to collect and charge for waste from a given locale, excluding all others. This leads to de facto monopolies and cherry-picking by the private sector, as they focus on the wealthier areas that are more likely to pay well, neglecting under-served informal communities and communal collection sites, which can often become mini-open dumpsites themselves. Weak enforcement of waste management laws by municipalities, even when there is an agreement to collect from communal areas, compounds this issue.

There is also a gender dimension to household waste management. Women often manage and dispose of household waste as well as overseeing household consumption. They are key to socializing children and normalizing the new habits and behaviours needed when introducing a new approach to waste management, although in many patriarchal societies they are not the final decision-makers (Ali, 2018).

Women often manage and dispose of household waste and oversee household consumption

Informal waste collectors are often the only provider of services in lower-income and informal settlements (Gunsilius et al., 2011). From the *borla-taxis* of Accra to the *pousse-pousseurs* of Kinshasa, there are numerous examples of local informal collection systems providing a service where no others will, at a price affordable to local people. However, some informal providers may also dump their waste openly or at illegal de facto dumpsites.

As the poor are less likely to have their waste collected, they bear the health, economic, and environmental costs most acutely, an obvious case of environmental injustice. Dumpsites tend to be located in or near lower-income communities, and those making a living from working from them tend to be the most marginalized (ISWA, 2016).

Informal workers in waste and recycling

Characterized by Wilson et al. (2006) as 'small-scale, labour intensive, largely unregulated and low-technology manufacturing or provision of services', the key driver of the informal waste sector is usually simple: to make money by sorting and selling recyclables. The field is dominated by families and microenterprises comprising women, children, and elderly relatives (Kaza et al., 2018). Broad categories of informal waste workers include those paid by businesses and householders to collect and transport residual waste; those collecting or buying certain materials for onward sale; and artisanal craftspeople turning recycled materials into saleable items (e.g. aluminium drinks cans into cooking pots).

A flourishing informal recycling sector depends on inadequate formal solid waste management, requiring uncontrolled access to dumpsites or openly dumped waste. Informal operators are only able to provide a service to households or businesses where regulations are loose enough to allow them to work without fear of prosecution.

Waste picking[1] is the first stage of the process where materials are collected from dumpsites or waste producers. It is often practised by marginalized groups, perhaps regionally or internally displaced peoples, or those from a certain ethnic or caste group, such as the Zabbaleen in Egypt or Dalit in India. Informal recycling is attractive because of the low barriers to entry and the comparatively high profit margins (Wilson et al., 2006).

The scale of the informal recycling sector

The number of people involved in the informal recycling sector is in the millions: a range of estimates suggest 2 per cent of the total global urban population in lower- and middle-income countries (Gunsilius et al., 2011), 15 million people worldwide (Velis, 2015); 1.5 million people in India (WIEGO, 2010); between 500,000 and 4 million people in Latin America (Marello and Helwege, 2014).

A recent study on the economic impacts of informal sector activities in six cities around the world (Cairo, Cluj, Lima, Lusaka, Quezon City, and Pune) found that all informal valorization generated a total net profit of €130 m, distributed between 73,000 informal workers (Gunsilius et al., 2011). In Bangladesh, the value of the informal sector is estimated to be US$173 m (Stevens et al., 2019).

Meanwhile, recycling recovery rates can be very high. For instance, the Zabbaleen group in Cairo have achieved rates of 80 per cent (see Box 2.2) due to a labour-intensive approach to collection and sorting and expertise at extracting value from waste (Gunsilius et al., 2011). This has led to the paradox that many cities in lower-income countries, without comprehensive waste collection, have higher recycling rates than their higher-income counterparts. Examples include Nairobi, where around 30 per cent of waste is recycled, or Quezon City where almost 40 per cent of waste is recycled (Fargier, 2015). This compares favourably with Rotterdam (23 per cent) and London (33 per cent) (SOENECS, 2017) and is delivered at little or no cost to the public purse.

> **Many cities in lower-income countries have higher recycling rates than in higher-income countries**

Challenges for informal waste workers

Informal waste workers can deliver transformative social benefits, but their welfare is all too often neglected: they generally do not pay taxes, are unlicensed, and work illegally, which means they are excluded from social welfare or government insurance schemes (Haan et al., 1998). Working with waste on a daily basis exposes them to multiple occupational hazards including pathogens, chemicals, and insanitary conditions, exacerbated if protective equipment and clothing is unavailable or unaffordable (Wilson et al., 2006). In a nationwide survey carried out in Bangladesh in 2019, 44 per cent of waste and sanitation workers said their work puts them at risk of injury (Stevens et al., 2019). Meanwhile, life expectancy of waste pickers can be much reduced – one study of waste pickers in Mexico City estimated life expectancy to be just 39 years against a citywide average of 67 years (Wilson et al., 2006).

They are also under threat from organized crime, with local criminals controlling access to dumpsites and extracting protection money, an example being Dandora dump in Nairobi (Muindi et al., 2016; Gumbihi, 2013). Meanwhile, formal waste collectors – licensed companies or municipal services – see them at best as an irritant and at worst as criminals. Chvatal (2010) describes how waste pickers in Western Cape, South Africa, were criminalized once they were banned from picking on the local landfills, leading to confrontation, violence, and murder (Kretzmann, 2020).

Informal recyclers face discrimination: they are seen as backwards, unhygienic, and not suited to a modern, clean urban environment (Wilson et al., 2006). The waste pickers of Mumbai were blamed for large and ongoing dump fires that led to smoke pollution throughout the city (Laskhmi, 2016). They are seen as unfair competition by the formal waste collectors, removing higher-value materials from within the waste stream (Wilson et al., 2006). In Bangladesh, 98 per cent of workers said they had experienced abuse or disrespect due to their work; families had been excluded from social events; they had difficulty in finding marriage partners for their children; and even their children struggled to find employment due to familial association (Stevens et al., 2019).

There is a widespread lack of economic mobility within the informal recycling sector, particularly for waste pickers. A lack of access to credit means they are unable to scale up. This makes them more vulnerable to exploitation from intermediate dealers as they cannot build up the resources to invest in scaling (Fergutz et al., 2011; Gunsilius et al., 2011).

Women waste pickers face even more challenges

Women play an important role within the informal recycling sector. In India, for example, about 80 per cent of waste pickers are women; in Thailand, about 93 per cent of street sweepers in the Bangsue district of Bangkok and 60 per cent of waste pickers at dumpsites are women (Hunt, 1996; Madsen, 2006; Dias and Fernandez, 2013). Women waste pickers face numerous challenges on top of the burden of hierarchical gender relations at home and in their respective communities. In Bangladesh, for example, a clear gender pay gap was reported, with male waste pickers earning around double that of women. They also faced specific occupational health risks, such as respiratory problems from street sweeping, with little consideration of needs during pregnancy or menstruation. Nearly half (42 per cent) said they continued working and doing heavy work even when pregnant, contrary to local employment laws. Early starting and late finishing and being alone in public spaces led to potentially risky situations and over a quarter of women complained of physical or sexual abuse (Stevens et al., 2019). Their livelihoods are also particularly vulnerable, as they often do the jobs that are disrupted by formalization and contracting out, such as street sweeping.

Informal recyclers are also vulnerable to the vagaries of the global recycling market. There is a greater demand for secondary materials in relatively industrialized countries such as Pakistan, as opposed to activity in less industrialized places (e.g. Somaliland). The unpredictability of incomes can be a major hindrance to economic mobility and one of the goals of those aiming to improve the economic agency of the informal sector is to provide more predictability in incomes (Plastics for Change offers one approach to this, see Box 2.5).

Despite the exclusion, harassment, discrimination, and poor working conditions they face, informal recyclers make a valuable contribution to the management of solid waste across the world. We need to value their contribution and knowledge and ensure that changes to waste collection and disposal systems build on it, supporting them to collect more material, more safely, and derive a better livelihood whilst doing it.

Waste: an inclusive urban resource economy?

The process of formalization of waste and recycling collection systems varies but often involves the fencing off of dumpsites and handing over of collection rights to one or more private or public sector organizations. This inevitably leads to conflict with the informal sector, who need access to dumpsites and collection points to harvest materials or move door-to-door to collect directly from households and businesses. This can also lead to lower collection coverage, as informal collectors often work in parts of towns and cities that are inaccessible to the vehicles of larger-scale operators, or because the local population is unable to pay their fees.

Waste and development – the traditional view

As a thematic area, solid waste has been grossly underfunded for years, with only 0.3 per cent of development aid going to solid waste management in 2012 (Lerpiniere et al., 2014). There has been an increase from this low base in recent years, notably from funds focused on addressing marine litter and plastic, such as the Global Plastic Action Partnership, the Commonwealth Clean Oceans Alliance, and a £500 m UK Government Blue Planet fund.

Historically, there has been a focus on treatment and containment of waste; technological solutions, in particular large-scale engineering projects; and support to middle-income countries (Lerpiniere et al., 2014), as well as numerous examples of inappropriate technologies. Medina (2007: 76) mentions the introduction of compactor trucks in cities which have streets that are too narrow and municipalities that have neither the finances nor technical capacity for maintenance, which includes failures of incinerator projects in large cities such as Manila, Istanbul, Lagos, Mexico City, and Surabaya. More recently, projects such as the Reppie incinerator in Addis Ababa have been accused of crowding out informal recyclers, targeting the same materials for combustion that they depend on for their livelihoods (Environmental Justice Atlas, 2019b).

One side-effect of this neglect is the poor quality of waste data, with a lack of empirical data on the impacts of mismanaged waste on human health and the environment (Godfrey, 2018). Whilst there are now more efforts to address this, again often focusing on leakage of plastics into the marine environment, this is in stark contrast to the wealth of data produced in, for instance, the WASH sector which benefits from networking and information-sharing structures to assist learning and improvement in project design.

Conventional solutions focus on large-scale engineering projects

Box 2.2 What happens if you try to get rid of the informal sector?

The Zabbaleen, translated as 'garbage people', are the traditional waste collectors of Cairo, Egypt. Coptic Christians in a largely Muslim society, they started collecting organic waste to feed to their pigs in return for a small monthly fee paid by residents. Over time, collection systems have become mechanized, and the service grew to include dry recyclables. In 2003, the Cairo Governorate decided to implement a policy of privatization of waste collection, preventing the Zabbaleen from collecting waste. Whilst the Zabbaleen had previously recycled 80 per cent, the new contractors were required to recycle only 20 per cent, the rest of which went to landfill. The Zabbaleen were offered jobs as waged workers with these companies. The salaries offered were lower than what they had made independently.

Citizens preferred the traditional door-to-door collection method of the Zabbaleen. Furthermore, the large vehicles of the private companies were unable to enter the narrow streets of Cairo, requiring the placement of bins in central collection points, leading to large amounts of open dumping.

Recycling rates collapsed, and the amount of waste sent to landfill increased. Traditionally, the Zabbaleen used to feed the organic waste to their pigs, but even this system stopped working when all their pigs were culled in 2009 by the government to avoid swine flu. With the main processor of organic waste gone, the Zabbaleen refused to collect organic waste from Cairo, leaving piles of garbage in the streets. Many Zabbaleen quit the recycling business as it became economically unviable without the rearing of pigs.

Source: adapted from the Environmental Justice Atlas (2019a)

Moving from waste to resource – the limitations of traditional approaches to waste management

The well-worn path of 'waste-development' observed by Whiteman et al. (2021) clearly has its limitations. The lag in the development of comprehensive, centralized municipal services has significant health and environmental consequences for local populations and, given the scale of urbanization, is now of global concern due to the potential adverse impacts of air pollution, marine plastics, public health, and climate change.

Waste collection coverage and the quality of governance within a city have been directly linked. It has even been proposed that the cleanliness of streets can be used as a simple indicator of the level of governance within a city (Whiteman et al., 2001). Approaches to funding waste management rely on strong cost recovery systems that are often lacking in the global South:

- Taxes (e.g. general taxes, taxes for other municipal services, property taxes) require a competent tax authority and mechanism to set realistic waste budgets. Whilst one advantage is that they can be universally collected, thus used to provide a 'free at the point of use' universal collection, they must be transparently allocated to waste services.

- · User charges, levied on various urban services or industrial services (e.g. industry charges, gate fees), can be collected either via ongoing charges or at the point of use. Whilst this is simple to administer and can work with public and large or small private sector companies, charges are often too high for those on low incomes, leading to open dumping in these communities.

Waste – the need for a new narrative

Whilst recognizing the roles of alternative models, particularly those operated by the informal sector, recent publications from the UN (for example the various *Waste Outlooks*) and the World Bank tend to take a view that there is a need for a large centralized authority and infrastructure. This is indicated in the structure of the reports themselves. *What a Waste 2.0* has five sections discussing waste governance, financing, and administration and one considering society, with a mere four pages (out of 184) considering the informal sector. There are several examples that take a different approach to the municipal or private sector model. A decentralized approach is one option. Godfrey (2018) considers the use of 'distributed grids' and notes that the usual level for decentralization is to local government level, although in some places where even this level of government functions poorly, such as rural Uganda, waste management takes place on a more local level, for instance on-site composting. A further example is outlined in Box 2.3.

Major global reports call for centralized infrastructure, and give little space to the informal sector

---

Box 2.3 Decentralized organic waste management by households in Burkina Faso

Cities in Burkina Faso are growing rapidly along with the amount of waste and the demand for agricultural products. To address these growing needs, the Ministry of Agriculture launched a Manure Pit Operation in 2001, inspired by the traditional practice of *tampouré*. Under this system, the government encourages households to establish pits and compost on their own land.

The government allocates funds each year to support household waste management. For example, between 2005 and 2012, the national government partnered with several development agencies to finance the construction of 15,000 manure pits in Burkina Faso's eastern region. Currently, about 2 million tonnes of organic fertilizer is produced in this way. A 2016 World Bank study revealed that 40 per cent of the total waste produced by households in secondary cities and peri-urban areas in Burkina Faso was directly processed on-site.

Source: Banna (2017)

Another question is how to develop comprehensive waste collection in an inclusive way. The example below of success from Pune municipality in India (see Box 2.4) shows one way forward, integrating informal workers into a formalized 'take everything' approach.

Meanwhile, there are other approaches, such as that of Plastics for Change, aiming to improve the economic agency of the informal sector by providing more predictable incomes (see Box 2.5).

Box 2.4 Integration of informal recyclers in Pune, India

In Pune, India, a cooperative of 3,000 waste pickers won better working conditions by joining forces with municipal authorities to collect waste door-to-door. In 1993 they organized themselves into the Kagad Kach Patra Kashtakari Panchayat union (KKPKP) and then campaigned to be recognized as workers. They underlined the benefits of what their members delivered for the city in terms of reducing waste disposal costs, creating jobs, and improving public health and the environment. In 2007 they set up a worker-owned cooperative of waste pickers, named SWaCH, providing front-end waste management services to Pune city, with support from the Pune Municipal Corporation.

The experience of the SWaCH model shows that informal waste workers are active and effective in recovering and valorizing resources, and this workforce-based approach can have positive economic, social, and environmental impacts. The informal waste pickers save an estimated US$12.5 m each year in labour, transportation, and processing costs, 46 per cent of the entire capital budget of Pune's solid waste management system. They also achieve considerable plastic recycling levels, with an estimated 30,000 tonnes of plastic sent annually for recycling, 52 per cent of the plastic waste in Pune. The annual greenhouse gas reduction from plastic waste diversion is estimated to be approximately 50,000 tonnes of CO_2 equivalent.

Source: adapted from WIEGO (2010)

Box 2.5 Fair prices for waste pickers: Plastics for Change and The Body Shop

Plastics for Change (PFC) partnered with local NGOs Hasiru Dala and Hasiru Dala Innovation to provide the waste pickers of the Indian city of Bengaluru with a stable income and better opportunities.

PFC developed an ethical sourcing platform to create sustainable livelihoods for the poor, helping wholesalers source plastic from waste pickers and gain access to high-value international markets by addressing three problems: (1) reducing volatility in price by facilitating long-term relationships with buyers who guarantee a fair minimum rate in advance; (2) providing access to working capital finance to ensure prompt payment can occur at the point of exchange throughout the supply chain; (3) preventing the exploitation of informal waste workers through a peer-to-peer rating and audit system.

PFC is now partnering with the UK retailer The Body Shop, which has started using plastics sourced through PFC to produce their 250 ml shampoo and conditioner bottles.

Informal recyclers and technology

The Fourth Industrial Revolution and globalization throw up opportunities and challenges for informal waste workers. On the one hand, the availability of cheap smartphones has seen the development of systems such as ScrapQ (see Box 2.6), that allow informal recyclers to work more efficiently and engage with new customers. On the other hand, automation could threaten much of the work of informal recyclers, which is labour intensive by its nature (Velis, 2017). Access to non-digital technologies, such as vehicles, shredders, and pelletizers can increase efficiency and turnover. However, it has been noted that credit is hard to come by and can lead to unaffordable loans and running costs. Ensuring access to cheap, robust equipment that can be maintained locally is vital (Casey, 2016).

Box 2.6 Uber for waste pickers: ScrapQ

ScrapQ, based in Hyderabad, India, is an app that acts as an aggregator to connect customers and the local *kabadiwala* (waste collectors). It operates like an 'Uber' for waste pickers with a network of 2,300 *kabadiwalas* serving more than 12,000 customers across the city. They have prices that fluctuate daily depending on world market prices, and they service households and businesses.

Whereas before, a kabadiwala would walk down the street calling for householders to bring out their recyclables, ScrapQ allows them to wait in the office, arrange a collection with the householder, and collect the materials at the agreed time. Payments are made via the ScrapQ app, avoiding the need to handle cash.

Summary

The challenge is to develop new, inclusive approaches to waste management that address the following issues:

- How do we accelerate the move towards comprehensive collection coverage for all sectors of the community within a town or city?
- How can we move straight to a position of comprehensive collection but also with high recovery rates?
- How do we ensure the most marginalized do not have their livelihoods harmed in the process, and the benefits of these secondary resources are shared equitably?

3 PEOPLE-CENTRED ASSESSMENT

Globally, there is very poor data availability on solid waste management. Few cities in the developing world have effective systems in place to measure and monitor basic metrics such as quantities of waste arriving at a disposal site. Where data is collected, the focus is on waste flows, rather than on the services people receive, or the extent to which neighbourhoods are free from waste. The contribution of the full range of service providers, including the informal sector, is often overlooked.

In this report, we use a people-centred approach to assessing waste management at the citywide level. We consider levels of service for communities, and the full range of service providers. We also adopt and adapt best practice tools. Our objectives are to show how a people-centred approach uncovers issues and priorities which are otherwise overlooked, and highlights new opportunities for addressing the situation.

Case study selection

We selected four varied towns and cities in different countries. Two are smaller secondary towns (Satkhira and Dhenkanal), one is a medium–large city (Kisumu), and one, a large capital city (Dakar). The resources channelled to waste management, opportunities in the waste trading economy, and the attitudes and expectations of stakeholders all differed. While the focus is often on metropolitan cities, smaller secondary towns are growing in number and size, and have fewer resources and lower capacities to ensure access to basic services for all. The four selected locations were:

1. **Dhenkanal** Municipality, Odisha State, India. Population 74,200, with around 16,670 in 43 slum communities. The town is centrally located in the eastern State of Odisha, surrounded by forest and agricultural land. It is one of 114 urban areas in the State.
2. **Satkhira** Municipality, Khulna Division, Bangladesh. Population 170,000 with around 17,000 living in 47 slum communities. The town is in the south-west of Bangladesh, just 15 km from the Indian border. It serves the surrounding agricultural area, with large businesses in fishing (shrimp cultivation), and trans-national trade with India.
3. **Kisumu** City, Kenya. Population 502,000 with around 301,000 living in low-income settlements. The city lies within the County of Kisumu (population 1.16 million), and is governed as a semi-autonomous body under the county government. Kisumu serves as a commercial and transport hub for the western part of Kenya.
4. **Dakar** City, Senegal. Population 2.88 million urban residents in the Dakar region, mostly in the districts of Dakar and Pikine. An estimated 25 per cent of the region's population fell below the poverty line in 2016 (ANSD, 2016). The city is the region's largest port for international trade and nodal hub for road infrastructure. It is the focus of the country's industrial, commercial, and financial activities.

Assessment tools and sampling strategies

The fieldwork tools we used drew on two recent guides: an early version of the Waste Wise Cities Tool (UN-Habitat, 2021) and guidance for the WasteAware indicators (Wilson et al., 2015). To ensure a people-focused analysis, we included a range of qualitative methods and survey questions exploring people's preferences and experiences.

In each city we used the following methods:

- Household questionnaire survey of a representative sample from areas defined as low income or slums, middle income, and high income. We analysed information by wealth category, and for the city as a whole by applying a weighting. Our sample (around 400 per city) was designed to achieve a confidence level of 95 per cent and a margin of error of 5 per cent. Within each household, we interviewed 'an adult who takes responsibility for dealing with the solid waste'.
- Questionnaire survey of around 20 service providers from four groups:
  - pickers, who recover recyclable items from waste dumped in neighbourhoods or at a dumpsite

We drew on the Waste Wise Cities Tool and the WasteAware indicators

– traders, who buy separated waste from pickers or collectors, sort it, sometimes do initial processing and sell in bulk
– collectors, who visit streets, households, and businesses removing mixed waste
– sweepers, who clear waste from streets and open spaces.

· A mapping exercise identifying waste hotspots in selected neighbourhoods.
· Focus group discussions and individual case study interviews with householders and service providers. Some of these were women-only groups to ensure gendered perspectives were heard effectively.
· Key informant interviews with decision-makers and service providers.
· A waste quantities and composition exercise collecting, weighing, and sorting waste from households in low-, middle-, and high-income neighbourhoods. Waste was collected for eight days, with the first day's waste discarded.

The sampling strategy for both the household survey and waste quantities and composition exercise varied slightly depending on the size and population distribution of the city (Table 3.1).

The sampling strategy and tools left some gaps in our ability to accurately map waste flows and calculate the quantities of waste recovered for recycling. The full version of the Waste Wise Cities Tool provides useful pointers which could be used to confirm the estimates we have made.

Table 3.1 Sampling strategy in each case study city

Dhenkanal, India	Satkhira, Bangladesh

Household survey of 406 stratified with
  142 in slum communities
  132 non-slum middle income
  132 non-slum higher income
Households were sampled from slum and non-slum communities across all wards in proportion to the population in each ward.
Waste quantities and composition survey:
  30 households – 10 each from slum, middle, and high income.
	Household survey of 402 stratified with
	  133 in slum communities
	  139 non-slum middle income
	  130 non-slum higher income
	Households were sampled from slum and non-slum communities across all wards and from randomly selected slum communities in each ward.
	Waste quantities and composition survey:
	  35 households – 15 from slum communities and 10 each from middle and high-income households.

Kisumu, Kenya	Dakar, Senegal

Household survey of 419 stratified with
  102 in Nyalenda A and 106 in Manyatta B low-income neighbourhoods
  108 in Migosi, a lower–middle-income area
  103 in Tom Mboya, a higher–middle-income area
Neighbourhoods were selected to be representative of the spread of wealth categories across the city.
Waste quantities and composition survey:
  90 households – 30 each from Nyalenda A, Migosi, and Tom Mboya.
	Household survey of 400 stratified with
	  100 in Pikine and 100 in Malika low-income settlements
	  100 in Cite Lobatt Fall, a middle-income area
	  100 in Point E, a high-income area
	Neighbourhoods were selected to be representative of the spread of wealth categories across the city.
	A waste quantities and composition survey was not carried out because data was available from a comprehensive 2014 study.

Table 3.2 Qualitative methods

Dhenkanal, India	Satkhira, Bangladesh

Focus groups involving 22 people
    Households: 3 groups, one women only
    Service providers: none
Case studies: 2 service providers
Key informant interviews: 5 people
	Focus groups involving 50 people
	    Households: 3 groups, all mixed, majority
	        women
	    Service providers: 3 groups, one men only
	Case studies: 7 people (householders and
	        service providers)
	Key informant interviews: 5 people

Kisumu, Kenya	Dakar, Senegal

Focus groups involving 41 people
    Households: 3 groups, one women only
    Service providers: 2 groups, one men only
Case studies: 5 people (householders and
        service providers)
Key informant interviews: 7 people
	Focus groups involving 57 people
	    Households: 4 groups, all mixed, majority men
	    Service providers: 4 groups, all mixed
	Case studies: 11 people (householders and
	        service providers)
	Key informant interviews: 4 people

Proposing a waste services ladder

Using our household survey, we analysed results to place each household on a ladder of waste services. The concept of a waste ladder is relatively new: first proposed by UN-Habitat in its Waste Wise Cities Tool (UN-Habitat, 2021). It is intended to mirror well-established ladders for water, sanitation, and hygiene (WHO and UNICEF, 2018). This ladder depends on an evaluation of the following factors:

1. *Access to a service*: The presence of a door-to-door waste collection service or designated collection point.
2. *Quality of the service*: The frequency and regularity of the collection service. For collection points, the frequency and regularity of emptying, distance from the household (> or < 200 m), and whether there is 'major littering' around the point.
3. *Separating waste*: Whether waste is collected (door-to-door or at the disposal point) in separate fractions (wet and dry, or in additional fractions of dry waste).

In our analysis, we tried applying UN-Habitat's ladder, but found that in some respects it did not adequately reflect the situations we found. We are therefore proposing two key changes. First, we added a separate category to capture the extent to which waste remains littering the neighbourhood and specifically the impact householders feel this is having. This expands on the existing ladder which only asks about littering at the collection point. We feel this is necessary because a good waste service should ensure both that waste is removed from households and cleared from streets and public spaces in the direct vicinity of the house. We felt that a household could not be described as having any more than a 'limited control' service while waste is having a 'significant' impact in the locality.

Second, the questions about waste separation for recycling in UN-Habitat's ladder assume that collection of all wastes will be done by a single service provider who will require waste to be separated into specified fractions. However, in most developing countries, informal traders collect waste fractions from households (metals, plastics, paper) even where the mixed-waste collection service does not require separation. This contribution is lost unless we broaden our definitions. We therefore asked whether separate fractions are collected from a household, not whether separation is required by mixed-waste collectors. We recognize that mixed-waste collection is the first necessary element of a good waste service, and therefore separation for recycling is factored into the ladder only in the upper two tiers.

Finally, we refined the definition of what it means to have a well-functioning and clean collection point. We broadened UN-Habitat's questions about 'littering' to ask whether the point is 'clean, safe, and with waste contained'.

The definitions for each level are described in Table 3.3, with our variations to UN-Habitat definitions in green. In summary, there are four factors that we considered in our adapted waste services ladder:

1. *Access to a service*: Whether households have access to a service where their mixed waste is removed either from their door or from a nearby disposal point.
2. *Quality of the service*: Whether the service is frequent and regular, and whether disposal points are well-managed.
3. *Impact of waste in the locality*: The extent to which waste is having an impact on the locality as a proxy to measure the degree of remaining littering of the streets.
4. *Separation for recycling*: Whether households separate waste fractions for recycling, irrespective of whether this is collected by a single, or multiple, service provider.

Table 3.3 Revised ladder of household waste services (variations to UN-Habitat definitions in green)

Service level	Definition
Full control	Receiving door-to-door municipal solid waste (MSW) collection service with basic frequency and regularity OR having a designated collection point within 200 m served with basic frequency and regularity / point described as clean, safe, and waste contained AND waste causing 'small' or 'no' impact in the locality AND at least one fraction of waste collected for recycling (in addition to mixed-waste collection)
Improved control	Receiving door-to-door MSW collection service with basic frequency and regularity OR having a designated collection point within 200 m served with basic frequency and regularity / point described as clean, safe, and waste contained AND waste causing 'small' or 'no' impact in the locality NO items separated for recycling
Basic control	Receiving door-to-door MSW collection service with basic frequency and regularity OR having a designated collection point within 200 m served with basic frequency and regularity / point described as clean, safe, and waste contained AND waste causing only 'moderate' or less impact in the locality
Limited control	Receiving door-to-door MSW collection service without basic frequency and regularity OR having a designated collection point within 200m but not served with basic frequency and regularity / point described as dirty, hazardous, or waste not contained OR having a designated collection point, but further than 200 m / having 'basic control' but waste causing 'significant impact' in the locality
No control	Receiving no waste collection service, or no collection point

WasteAware indicators and a people-centred approach

The WasteAware indicators and their associated user guide (Wilson et al., 2015) have been tested in several global cities. They are designed to be applicable in both developed and developing world contexts and in both small and large urban areas. They aim to help 'assess the performance of the municipal solid waste management and recycling system ... in a standardized manner' (Wilson et al., 2015). The indicators give a score from 'low' to 'high' based on both quantitative and qualitative assessments. We concentrate here on the scores for physical components (seven indicators) and governance factors (five indicators). Of these, three are quantitative and nine are composite indicators with a score built up from a set of subjectively scored sub-indicators.

Overall, we found the indicators useful in giving a rounded impression of the waste management system. However, there were occasions where overall scores did not reflect the diversity of experience for different communities or stakeholders. For example, there is a sub-indicator as part of measuring 3R, the quality of reduce, reuse, recycle provision, which asks about the 'use of appropriate personal protection equipment and supporting procedures'. There can be quite good compliance among formal service providers, but no or low compliance among informal service providers.

Secondly, we note that the composite indicators can bury the important role of the informal sector and inequalities in access to services in low-income areas. Our intention with this report is to shine a light on these differences.

Finally, while understanding that the indicators are geared to municipal-level performance, it is a weakness that they do not address gender inequalities in any of the indicators or guidance. Our findings reveal that there can be important ways in which women experience discrimination both in terms of the impacts of poor service delivery and as service providers themselves.

> The WasteAware indicators could be improved to better reflect diverse experiences within a city

Conclusion

Our overall approach is to use a set of methods and tools which provide an accurate picture of the waste management situation at the citywide level, while also putting people back at heart of the narrative. This includes paying attention to inequalities as they exist between neighbourhoods and between women and men, and to waste services as much as waste flows. We used best practice tools, adapting them where we felt necessary and highlighting where there are shortcomings. We welcome further discussion about how to refine tools and analysis to put people and the services they receive at the centre.

4 SATKHIRA, BANGLADESH

Bangladesh is a densely populated country which continues to urbanize. Between 2015 and 2020 the urban population grew by 17 per cent, while the rural population shrank by 1 per cent. In 2014, an estimated 23,688 tonnes of municipal solid waste were generated every day, an amount predicted to rise to 47,000 tonnes by 2025 (Waste Concern, 2016). This includes an increase in average waste generated per person, associated with a growing economy. As most of this waste continues to be openly dumped or taken to landfill, there will continue to be increased greenhouse gas emissions from waste.

Local authorities in Bangladesh are mandated to address solid waste management. A national 3Rs strategy (2010) encourages them to reduce, reuse, and recycle, rather than simply focusing on collection and disposal. The seventh national five-year plan (2015–2020) also promoted a 3Rs strategy. Despite a range of initiatives, the national government recognizes that there remains a lack of capacity, technology, and financial resources to implement the strategy effectively (GoB, 2019). Bangladesh's national commitments to the Paris Climate Change Agreement included the commitment that '50 per cent of the managed waste fraction should be

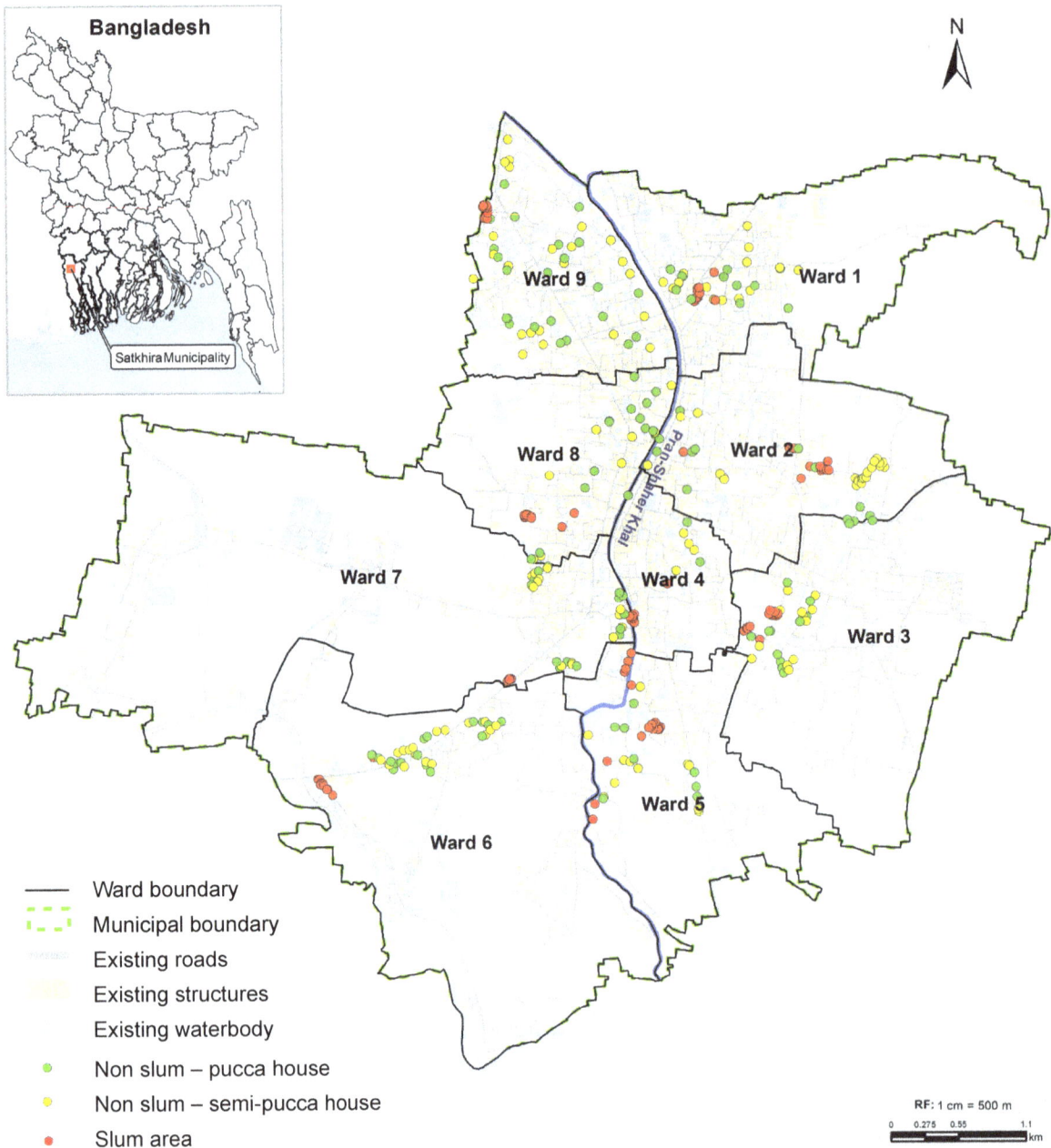

Figure 4.1 Distribution of household survey points

diverted from landfill to composting', but this was 'conditional' on securing additional external financing (MOEF, 2015).

Satkhira Municipality: background and waste management structures

Satkhira is one of 328 *Pourashavas* (municipalities) in Bangladesh. With an estimated population in 2020 of 169,991 in 34,939 households, it is in the largest 15 per cent of all the municipalities in the country. The town is in the south-west of Bangladesh, and is one of 21 category A municipalities in Khulna Division. There are an estimated 47 slum communities, home to 17,064 people (10 per cent of the population). These are in relatively small pockets of between 12 and 300 households (median of 50). As a proxy for relative wealth in the town, 40 per cent of all households live in *pucca* structures. The rest (including slum dwellers) are in *semi-pucca* or *katcha* housing (Practical Action, 2016). We used these proportions to weight the findings from our household survey.

A large drainage canal, the Pran-Shaher Khal, runs through the centre of the town. During the monsoon, many places in the district, including the town, suffer from prolonged waterlogging. Satkhira town serves the surrounding agricultural area and trans-national trade, with the Indian border just 15 km away.

The Conservancy Department of the municipality is responsible for solid waste management. The department has two supervisors and a team of 113 street sweepers and drivers who focus on clearing waste from the streets and communal bins in both the town centre and residential areas. They operate with a small fleet of vehicles: three trucks and seven smaller vehicles.

The department also manages a disposal site about 5.5 km from the centre of the town. This site is not well managed, not fenced, surrounded by water bodies, and with settlements nearby. There is no data management or monitoring at the site. Waste is simply dumped and flattened with tractors. This is reflected in a 'low' score for the quality of environmental protection in final disposal in the WasteAware indicators (2E).

Household access to waste services

The municipality teams operate in all wards except two that are largely rural. They have provided six larger waste collection points and 80 concrete dustbins where people are meant to bring their waste. It provides a collection service to 1,800 households (5 per cent). In addition, a handful of small businesses (four to five) provide a collection service (see Figure 4.9 at the end of the chapter). Our waste ladder considers four key elements of service provision:

1. *Access*: The vast majority of households in the town, 84 per cent, have no waste service. They have no collection service, nor do they use the municipality's communal bins. They leave their waste on a street corner, drain, or other open area. Some households bury their waste, and a small minority burn it. Only 6 per cent of households have a door-to-door collection service (none in slum areas), and 10 per cent use a formal disposal point. Only 11 per cent of residents mentioned any neighbourhood clean-up efforts, even irregularly.
2. *Quality*: Where people use a disposal point, it is more than 200 m away (for 75 per cent who use one) or dirty and hazardous, or waste is not contained (for half of those who use one).
3. *Impact*: Despite the lack of services, households tended not to rate the 'impact that indiscriminate waste dumping is having in our area' as severe: around a quarter of people overall, but rising to 40 per cent in slum communities (Figure 4.2).
4. *Separation for recycling*: Waste separation for recycling is very common in Satkhira, with 84 per cent of households separating out at least one type of waste for recycling. The practice of recycling is lower among slum communities (75 per cent). However, this does not solve the problem most people have of what to do with the bulk of their waste.

Overall, households are poorly served in terms of waste management in the town. Slum areas are the least well served, while there are no significant differences in services by wealth category in non-slum areas (see Figure 4.5 at the end of this chapter).

The vast majority of households in the town have no waste service

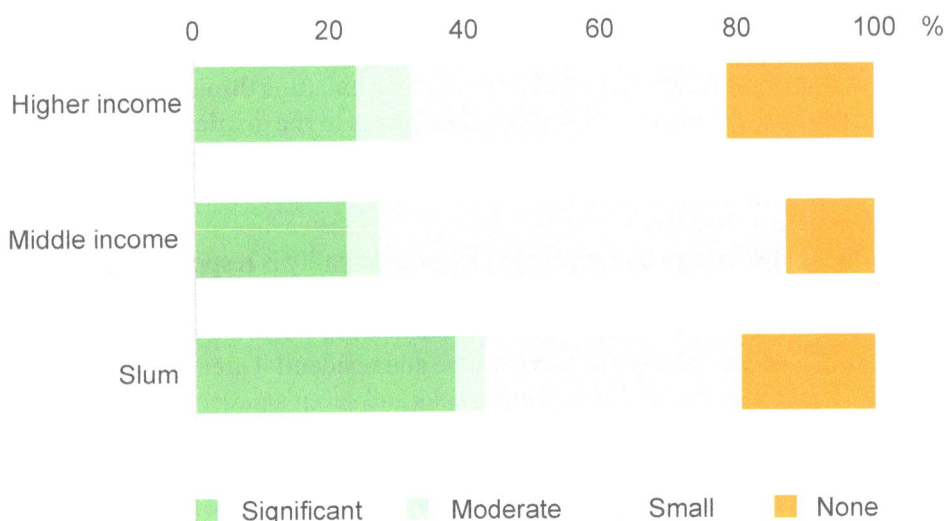

Figure 4.2 Perception of impact of solid waste disposal in the neighbourhood

Elaborating on the impact of poor waste management, the top three problems in our survey were the smell, blocked drainage, and waste attracting flies and mosquitoes. The problems were most acute during the rainy season. The focus groups and individual interviews highlighted how these issues are connected. Participants (majority women) from one slum community described how, in the rainy season, all the drains overflow, spreading water and waste across the whole area, including into their courtyards. All year round, the piles of waste in drains, ponds, and open spaces attract 'increased infestations of mosquitoes, flies, insects, and spiders'. Even during light rains, roads are waterlogged because the drains are blocked. Spaces where children can play are ruined and become dangerous because of the piles of waste. The participants linked these issues to increased rates of sickness. The women talked about the stress and 'unbearable stench' caused by a combination of waterlogging and heavy pollution with solid waste (Figure 4.3).

Responsibilities for waste management at the household level are gendered. Focus group participants explained it is usually the oldest woman who takes care of solid waste management, because they are responsible for the home and kitchen. However, financial decisions fall to the household head (male, or jointly male and female). In our survey, women consistently reported the impact of poor waste management as more severe than reported by men. In slum communities, over half the women (55 per cent) said that poor waste management was a leading issue for them that affected their day-to-day activities, while two-thirds (66 per cent) of men said it was 'not an issue of concern' for them.

An unbearable stench is caused by waste combined with waterlogging

Household waste composition

We found that 79 per cent of household waste in Satkhira is organic, very similar to the *pourashava* average found by Waste Concern (2016) of 78 per cent. The remainder included plastics: 2 per cent was thin film and 5 per cent was dense plastics. Another 6 per cent was textiles (see Figure 4.6).

We asked service providers whether they had noticed a change in waste types or quantities over the past year during the COVID-19 pandemic. Out of 20, 18 said there had been no noticeable changes, and the two sweepers who noticed changes did not refer to items we might associate with the pandemic (increased plastic wrappings or items such as face masks).

Around 56 tonnes of waste is generated per day in Satkhira

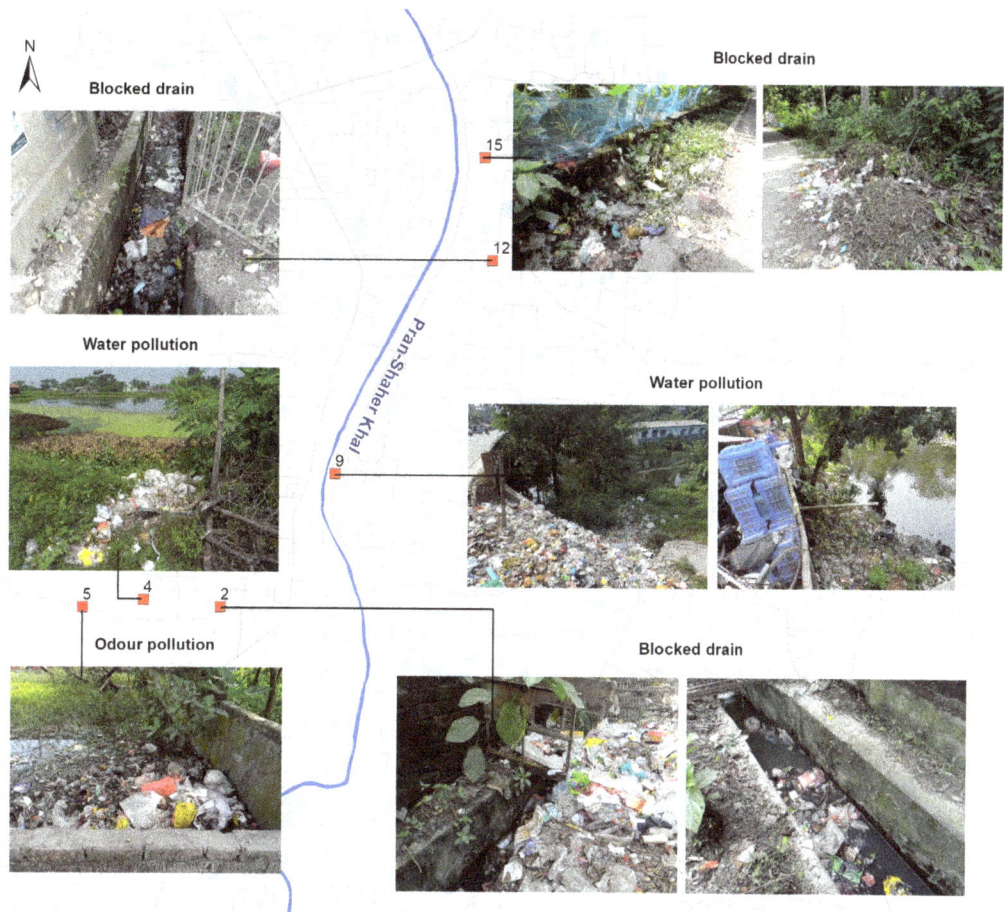

Figure 4.3 Negative impacts of waste

Waste service providers

The average quantity of waste per person per day in Satkhira is low by global standards at only 0.25 kg (Figure 4.7 at the end of the chapter). Overall, this means that, together with commercial and institutional waste, around 56 tonnes per day is generated. There are no clear estimates of the number of people working in waste businesses in the town, but there are likely to be at least 400, based on estimates for other towns.[1]

One of the most striking things about waste management in Satkhira is the proportion of households that reported separating out at least one type of waste (Figure 4.4). This is dominated by plastics, with 69 per cent of respondents separating these because they can sell them (93 per cent), or they are collected from their home (6 per cent). The second most commonly household-separated waste is paper or cardboard (37 per cent). This recycling is supported by a network of waste pickers, collectors, and traders. For these service providers, the most valuable waste is metal, followed by (rigid) plastics and paper/cardboard.

This contribution means that potentially 441 tonnes of plastics, 78 tonnes of paper, and 52 tonnes of metal are being recovered every year.[2] And this is being achieved completely without any public sector intervention. On the other hand, these waste fractions only make up 8 per cent by weight of the household waste stream.

This thriving and extensive ecosystem of material recovery is predominantly informal. None of the waste collectors or pickers was registered, and only two out of five waste traders were. Only one out of 20 workers belonged to an association: one of the sweepers, who was also the

This thriving ecosystem of material recovery is predominantly informal

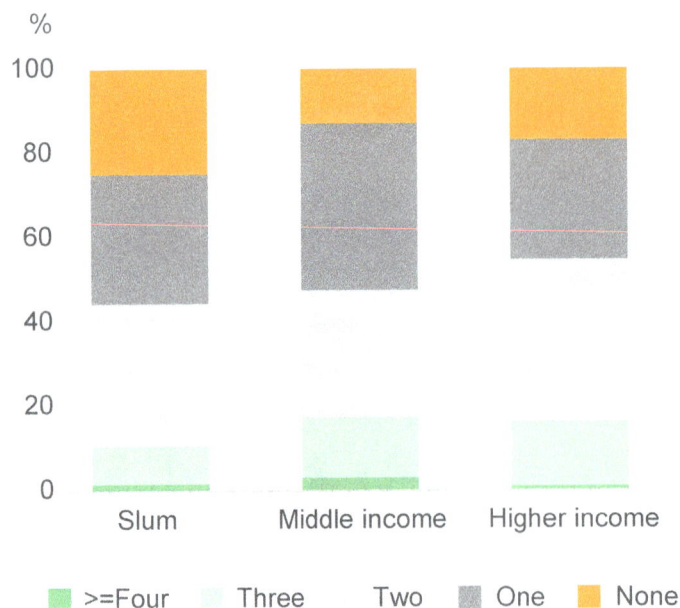

Figure 4.4 Number of items separated by households for recycling

only one who had received any training. Hardly any had a relationship with the municipality (only one waste trader).

The sector is heavily male dominated, except for those employed by the municipality as street sweepers (35 women and 10 men). Waste traders tended to be older (mostly over 40 years) and were slightly better educated, mostly having primary schooling, while all the pickers and most of the sweepers did not have even a primary education.

Waste pickers and collectors

Private waste collectors have operated in Satkhira for a number of years: all those we interviewed had operated for between three and eight years. However, they remain small-scale, serving only up to 10 households each (one served up to 20) on an 'on demand' basis, rather than regularly. The collectors make additional money by selling recyclables from the waste they collect. Waste pickers had worked for a similar length of time (three to six years), selling what they pick to traders. They operate both at the final disposal point and within the town.

Waste traders

The waste traders estimate that there are around 120 businesses working in waste trading. They buy waste door-to-door, or from collectors and pickers. The aggregated waste is sold on to traders in larger urban centres: Khulna, Jessore, or Dhaka. One mentioned that to grow requires 'more investment in warehouse space, transport, a weighing machine etc.', which is only built up over time. At the same time, a larger operation means greater requirements for licensing, fees, and acquiring land. Some felt expansion was blocked by 'a syndicate of larger firms controlling opportunities with bribes and political influence'.

Around 120 businesses are working in waste trading

> ### Box 4.1 Case study: Praveen Khatun, waste picker
>
> Praveen works with her husband in the business. Every day they collect a minimum of 5–7 kg and sometimes as much as 10–12 kg of waste, using their van to sell the waste to traders. They have been able to pay off debts accumulated from a previous less successful business.
> 'We are happy with this business', she said. She recognizes there are risks of injury, and her work would be easier if people kept their waste separate, so it is easier to collect.

Municipal services including sweepers

With its workforce of sweepers, collectors, and drivers, and a small fleet of vehicles, the municipality clears waste from major roads and markets three times a week and secondary roads twice a week.[3] The conservancy officer reports that about 16 tonnes of waste per day is taken to the final disposal site. This represents around 30 per cent of the total.

Sweepers say they do not have permanent contracts with the municipality. They work from 5 or 6 a.m. until between 10 a.m. and 12 noon for a monthly wage of 2,900 BDT[4] or US$34. They make a little extra money picking out recyclables to sell to waste traders (three of the five we interviewed).

Working conditions, harassment, and discrimination

The most common problems mentioned by pickers and collectors were a lack of access to PPE (mentioned by six out of 10), although most do wear boots and gloves. Waste traders also mentioned facing health risks and needing easier access to PPE. Being a sweeper was also not a safe or desirable job, and women in the focus groups said people only came to it out of desperation. Pay is low and conditions are difficult. Roadside restaurants and shops refuse to serve them during their working hours, and they have no access to water, toilets, or handwashing facilities. They are provided with PPE equipment but find it extremely hot.

Pickers and collectors were the most likely to be harassed at work. Women sweepers equally faced harassment and felt unsafe, especially when starting work very early in the morning. Waste traders in the focus group explained that they risk being accused of, or unwittingly, handling stolen goods. At the same time, in our household survey, the majority (68 per cent) recognized that waste pickers are doing a good job. Very few (5 per cent) thought they caused problems.

Some efforts have been made recently to improve conditions, in particular for sweepers. Practical Action Bangladesh started an association (one of the five sweepers we interviewed belonged). Focus group participants also belonged to this association, and were aware of a health insurance scheme that was being established.

Voluntary community action

The example shown in Box 4.2 (next page) is unusual. One of the women we interviewed had been trying to motivate her neighbours to clean up their area and lead by example. She said, 'No one came out with a supportive attitude and responded'. She did, however, successfully persuade the municipality to provide street sweepers in her area (which had not been served before). The (male) leader of a local mosque had more success in

Waste pickers and collectors are often harassed while working

motivating his neighbours to help keep the area around the mosque clean saying, 'When I have started doing the cleanliness activities by my own, one of the positive signs was that people around me came forward to help'.

Box 4.2 Case study: Local resident takes action

'Presently, all the households that are living in this locality are dumping their household waste everywhere and as a result the entire areas become a dirty place and bad odours are also polluting the surrounding areas' [English Teacher, Ward 1]. He personally took the initiative to photograph the situation and post those photos to the mayor's Facebook page. He bought bins and distributed them around the area, and persuaded the mayor to contribute bins and ensure waste is collected. Ward 1 is now one of the three wards that has higher access to disposal points than elsewhere (13 per cent of households).

In our household survey, nearly three-quarters (74 per cent) felt that it was not acceptable to throw waste on the street: a view shared equally by men and women. At the same time, 19 per cent said, 'It's fine, it's someone else's job to keep things clean', with the better-off more likely to hold this attitude. As a local woman activist said, 'People living in the area are financially rich and education levels are very high, but, their waste management awareness is very low... They throw their household wastes here and there without any hesitation' [Ward 2, housewife and community worker].

Governance and regulation

The WasteAware indicators provide an overview of how well the city is performing (Figure 4.8). We have noted that national policies exist to promote recovery and recycling, and to divert waste from landfill. However, in secondary towns like Satkhira, it is hard to make this a reality. Solid waste management is significantly under-resourced in terms of staffing, equipment, and budget. The budget covers at best half (probably an

The budget
available covers
at best half of
what it costs
to provide
a collection
service

under-estimate) of what it would cost to provide a collection service to everyone and adequate street sweeping. This budget comes from a service charge paid by householders and businesses (but not those living in slums). The municipality has no solid waste strategy, plan, or targets, and has not considered how to cope with growing amounts of waste as the population grows year by year. This is reflected in low and low-medium scores for local institutional coherence (6L) and financial sustainability (5F).

One area where the municipality does better is on user inclusivity (4U). Perhaps thanks to the efforts of local civil society and a number of governance-related projects over time, the town has functioning multi-stakeholder ward-level and town-level coordination committees. These committees include community representatives and often issues of solid waste management are raised.

On the other hand, waste traders and businesses, even the few who are formally registered, report that they are not engaged at all with the municipality (4P). They feel their expertise could help shape a joint strategy to improve the waste management situation, but there have been no opportunities to do so. There is an association of these businesses, but it is not currently active. One larger business owner said, 'Under the present practice, the businessmen only go to the municipal office for issuing or renewing the trade license in each year. [We don't] have any interaction with the municipal authority to discuss about business development, safety, security, or potential aspects of the waste management sector'.

Conclusion

The municipality recognizes that the solid waste management situation in the town is poor and that it needs to take action. However, they have found it difficult to imagine how to improve the situation within the scope of their limited resources.

Households are keen to have regular, convenient services which effectively remove all the waste from their neighbourhood. Most feel the municipality should be able to provide this based on the service charges they already pay. They are not keen to have more secondary collection bins. Communities have refused to allow additional bins in their area. This is probably a wise decision as they fear it will be as poorly managed as the others they already see.

Waste businesses and the informal sector would like to work in partnership with the municipality to devise a strategy. This should build on the existing strengths and practices where households are already used to separating out waste for recyclers. The extent of the recovery system for some more valuable types of waste is remarkable. There is clearly need for a significant awareness campaign around the contribution of waste workers, and the responsibilities of residents to do their bit to reduce waste problems. This campaign should recognize the highly gendered nature of waste management practices at the household level.

The town of Satkhira is continuing to grow. Its current waste management approach leaves increasing volumes of waste to rot, which pollutes the environment, risks the health of its citizens, and exacerbates problems of flooding and waterlogging. The national government's good intentions now need to be turned into a more active strategy, with greater financial support, incremental targets, and an approach to partnership which can harness existing strengths of the informal recycling sector. Every effort must be made to ensure that, in the process, the lives of informal waste workers and, in particular, women are uplifted.

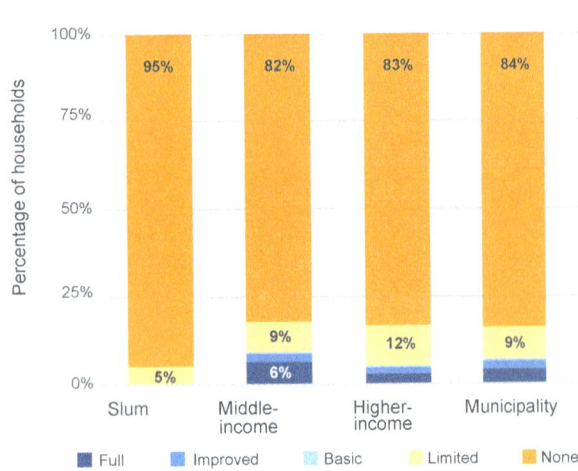

Figure 4.5 Waste services ladder by wealth category

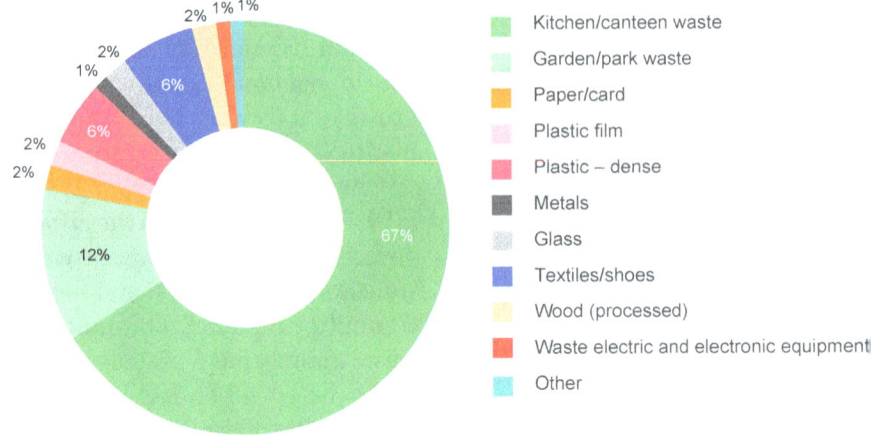

Key: Full, Improved, Basic, Limited, None

Figure 4.6 Composition of household waste, whole municipality

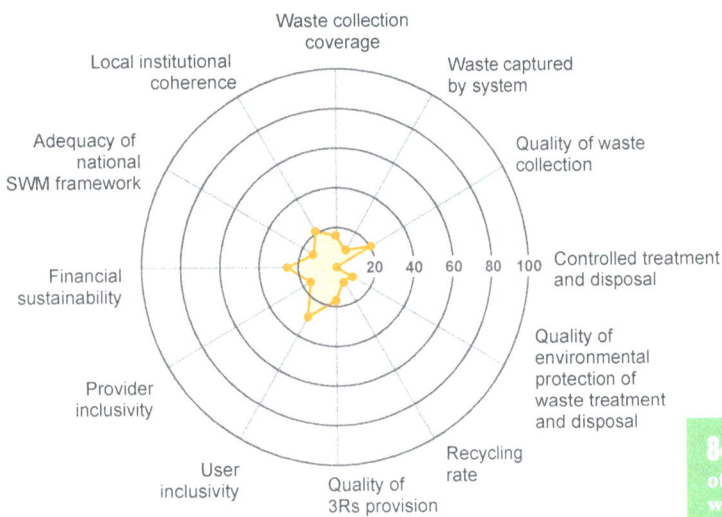

- Kitchen/canteen waste
- Garden/park waste
- Paper/card
- Plastic film
- Plastic – dense
- Metals
- Glass
- Textiles/shoes
- Wood (processed)
- Waste electric and electronic equipment
- Other

Figure 4.8 WasteAware indicators

0.27 KG Slums   **0.23 KG** Middle income   **0.26 KG** Higher income   **0.25 KG** Average for whole town

Figure 4.7 Average weight of waste per person per day

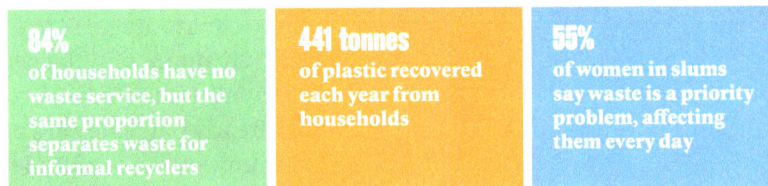

84% of households have no waste service, but the same proportion separates waste for informal recyclers

441 tonnes of plastic recovered each year from households

55% of women in slums say waste is a priority problem, affecting them every day

Figure 4.9 Municipal waste flows

WASTE GENERATORS 56

Large vehicle collection service 1,800 households

Mixed waste collection service from 300 households by 5 businesses

Door-to-door collection of recyclables from 29,300 households

Uncollected waste dumped on open ground, drains, river

Waste taken to disposal points

Waste swept by 113 municipal sweepers and drivers

Private sorting, trading, recycling – 120 businesses

Waste picked from street dumps

Binerpota dumpsite 16

Pickers recover recyclables

Remains uncollected on streets

Key:
- Tonnes per day
- Private service providers
- Municipal/public services

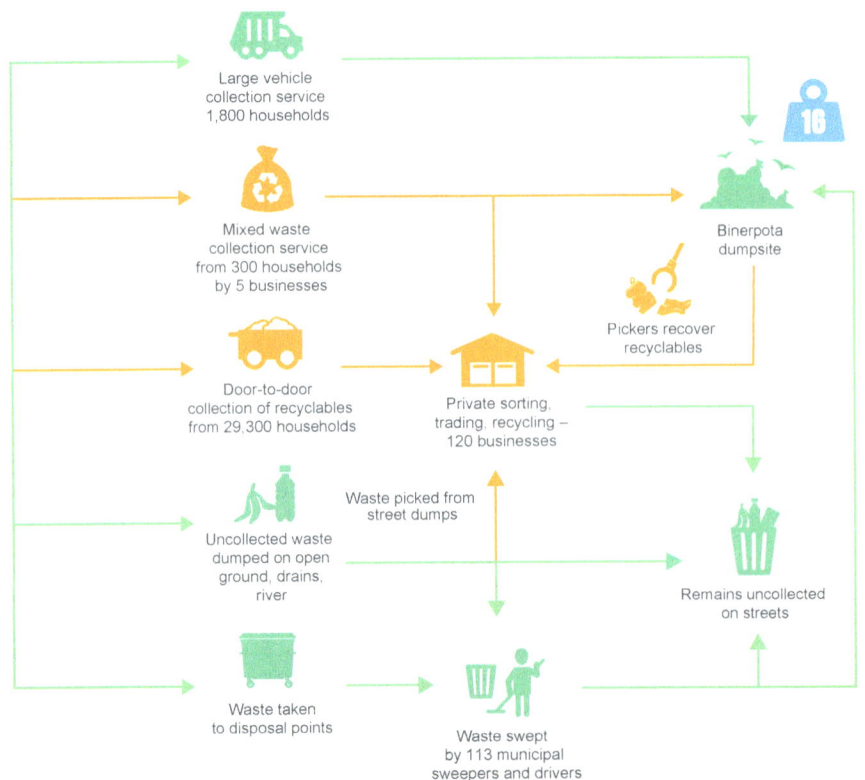

5 DHENKANAL, ODISHA, INDIA

The Indian urban population continues to grow, and with it enormous amounts of solid waste. As the *Asia Waste Management Outlook* (Modak et al., 2017: 7) highlights, 'consumerism in Asia is increasing at a rapid pace ... with higher material consumption of lifestyle products, food and beverages, electronics, etc.'. The capacity to deal with this is not developing fast enough. The national Ministry of the Environment, Forestry and Climate Change (MoEFCC) estimates that 75–80 per cent of municipal waste gets collected but only 22–28 per cent is processed and treated (Singh, 2020).

There have been efforts to strengthen legislation around solid waste management at the federal level. In 1996, public interest litigation in the Indian Supreme Court demanded that waste management should be hygienic and eco-friendly in all of India's Class-1 cities (populations over 100,000). Municipal Solid Waste Management rules direct municipalities to 'promote recycling or reuse of segregated materials' and 'ensure community participation in waste segregation'. From 2014 the Government's flagship Swachh Bharat (Clean India) Mission included an objective to ensure door-to-door waste collection and proper disposal by 2019 (Ghosh, 2016). New Solid Waste Management rules in 2016 encourage source segregation and the inclusion of informal waste pickers (Singh, 2020).

At the same time, waste picking is an established urban survival tactic, and recycling is a flourishing business across India's towns and cities. Some estimates are that it supports up to 0.5 per cent of the population in cities over 1 million inhabitants (Singh, 2021), and saves 10–15 per cent of total waste management costs incurred by city authorities. However, the integration of this informal sector with public sector processes is often weak, with only a few successful examples across the country (such as in Pune; see Parsons et al., 2019).

Dhenkanal Municipality: background and waste management structure

The success of solid waste management efforts in any given Indian town or city depends on the approach of the state and the capacity of the urban local government. Our study focused on the town of Dhenkanal in Odisha State, one of the states with the worst records on access to urban services at the time of the last census in 2011. Dhenkanal is one of 114 urban areas in the state. Its population was 67,414 in 2011, and is estimated to have grown by 10 per cent to 74,000 by 2021. The district contains large areas of forest and agricultural land. The town acts as the district headquarters, and is proud of its cultural heritage of ancient temples, a medieval fort, and popular annual festivals.

The local government estimates that as of 2020 there were 43 slum communities in the town, home to 16,670 people (just under a quarter of the population). Slums are relatively small, with an average (median) of 70 households. In our survey we sampled slum and non-slum households across all 23 municipal wards (Figure 5.1).

Solid waste management is the responsibility of the Municipal Engineer, working with an officer from the sanitation section. In 2015, door-to-door collection services were serving only some households, no waste segregation was being practised, and the final dumpsite was very poorly managed. Overflowing bins were common in markets and public places, and uncollected waste was creating a serious health hazard (Practical Action, 2015). In August 2019, the municipality launched a major solid waste management (SWM) drive. They signed a public–private partnership agreement (PPP) with Pratyush Sanitation to supervise and deliver collection services, and to operate new material recovery and micro-composting centres. Municipal staff still collect waste in eight wards. We collected data in December 2020, a little over a year since this service had begun to operate.

Household access to waste services

Since 2019, door-to-door collection services and street sweeping cover all wards of the town, serving slum and non-slum communities alike. The municipality directly employs 12 supervisors, 10 drivers, and more than 60 street sweepers. Pratyush employs 220 people as collectors, sweepers and labourers, drivers, and supervisors (Table 5.1). Source separation into wet (organic, kitchen waste) and dry fractions is encouraged. There is no accurate estimate of the numbers involved in informal waste trading, but it could be at least 300 people.[1] Together, they deal with the approximately 32 tonnes of waste generated every day. Our waste ladder considers four key elements of service provision for households:

32 tonnes of waste is generated in the town every day

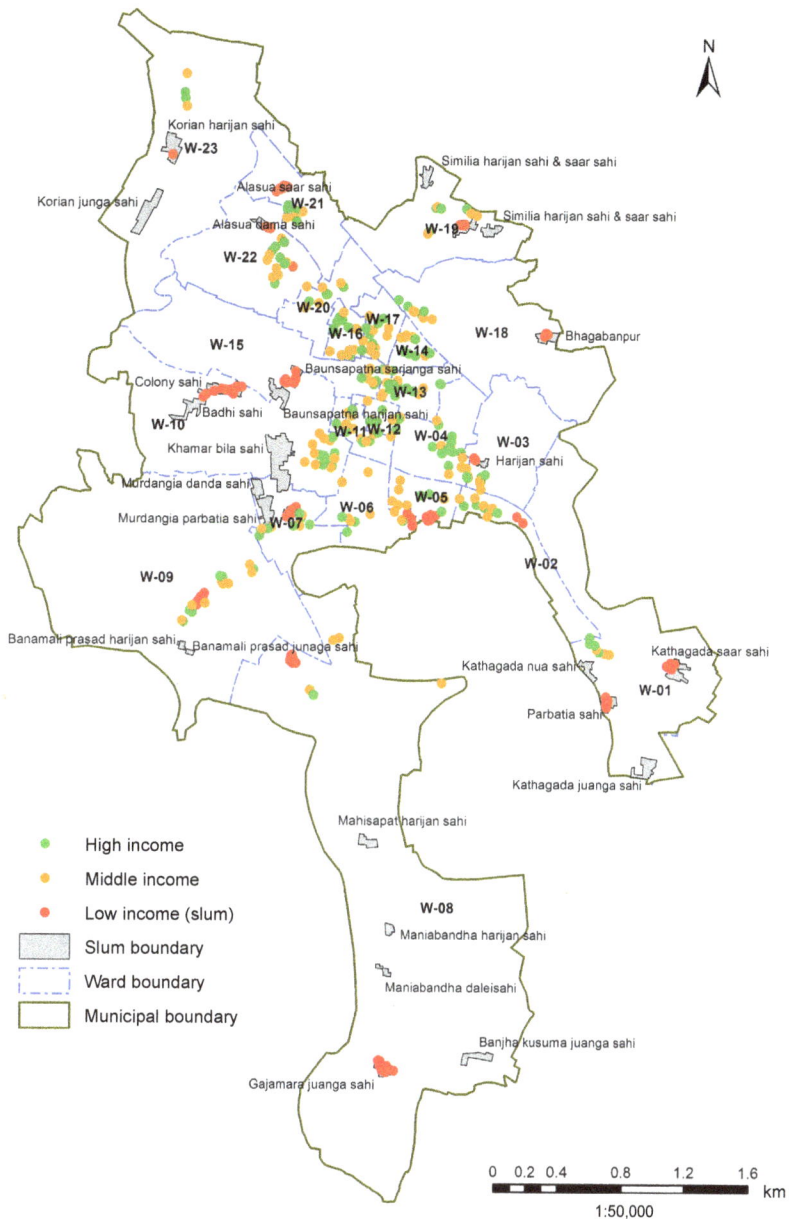

Figure 5.1 Map of household survey points for Dhenkanal Municipality

Waste collection services reach 97% of households

1. *Access:* The transformation brought by the PPP with Pratyush has been dramatic, with 97 per cent of households saying their waste is collected. Only four wards had rates below 100 per cent. A very small minority still resort to burning or disposing waste outside the home. Households are charged a fee by the municipality which varies depending on the plinth size of the house. On average this was Rp 22 per month in slum areas, Rp 45 for middle-income, and Rp 60 for higher-income households. This compares to the official daily minimum wage for unskilled labour in Odisha of Rp 303 in April 2020.

2. *Quality:* There were high levels of satisfaction with the reliability and overall quality of service for waste collection: 98 per cent said waste was collected as scheduled 'almost all of the time'. Waste is collected daily (98 per cent), public bins are emptied, and streets are swept.

3. *Impact:* Despite collection rates, people still reported that 'indiscriminate solid waste disposal' was having a negative impact in their neighbourhoods. In slum areas, this was 'moderate'

(94 per cent), and in non-slum areas it was 'significant' for 78 per cent. Respondents complained about blocked drains, pests (flies, mosquitoes, and rodents), and foul smells. They identified local markets as the main cause of the problem, along with, to a lesser extent, households, hotels, and cafes.

4. *Separation for recycling:* Waste is meant to be separated by households into wet and dry fractions for collection. Households also separate waste to sell to informal waste traders. In our survey, only 20 per cent of residents (10 per cent in slums and 22 per cent in non-slum communities) said they separate items for recycling: most commonly paper or cardboard, and organics/kitchen waste. It was not clear whether this was for waste traders, or the municipal waste collection service. Service providers confirmed that separation for municipal waste collection is not being done properly. Our estimate is that, with some potential confusion in survey responses, around 40 per cent of households are separating their waste.

Attitudes to litter remain quite poor despite recent awareness campaigns. In slum communities, two-thirds said that throwing litter on the street was fine because it was 'someone else's job to keep things clean'. Only 8 per cent of slum dwellers and 33 per cent of non-slum dwellers said littering was bad and everyone should take responsibility for keeping their area clean.

Overall, households are well served in terms of waste management. The ongoing impact of waste in the community, and the lack of separation for recycling, however, keeps households at the basic or limited level on the ladder (see Figure 5.3 at the end of the chapter).

Elaborating on the impact of poor waste management, focus groups and individual interviews highlighted the need for a good combination of collection services, emptying of public waste bins, and street sweeping. In focus groups, participants highlighted problems of smells, and pests such as rodents and other animals (dogs and cattle). One slum resident said 'we often see the waste bin is full and waste is overflowing. Sometimes ... a portion of the waste is littered around the bin. It's smelly, and a large open bin'. In the survey, blocked drains were the most commonly mentioned problem (Figure 5.2).

However, recent service improvements are beginning to change practices. Focus group participants commented, 'The municipality is doing a good job nowadays. To match that, families here are cooperating in every aspect of solid waste management'.

Management of waste at the household level is seen as women's work, as they are also the ones in charge of the house and kitchen. A higher proportion of women than men stay at home and manage the house. However, it is the male members of the household that are earning who pay for waste management services.

Household waste composition

The average quantity of waste per person per day was 0.33 kg in Dhenkanal (Figure 5.5). The majority of this was organic kitchen or garden waste (57 per cent). Other significant fractions include dense plastics, making 20 per cent of the waste, and paper or card, making 13 per cent (Figure 5.4). Service providers noted that waste had increased over the last year (during COVID-19), with some noting an increase in plastics as part of this.

Attitudes to litter remain quite poor despite awareness campaigns

The average quantity of waste per person per day was 0.33 kg

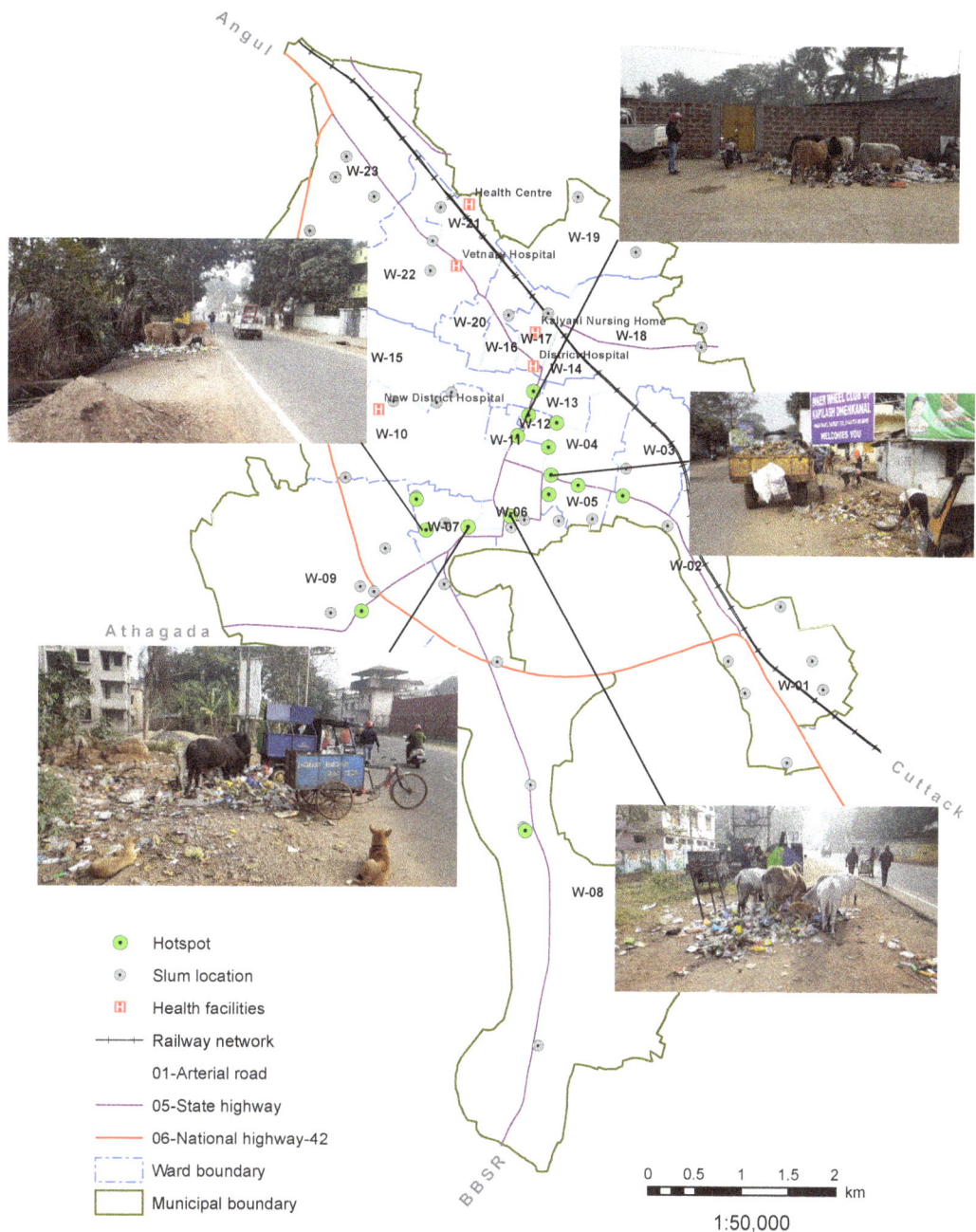

Figure 5.2 Waste management hotspots in Dhenkanal Municipality

Map legend:
- Hotspot
- Slum location
- Health facilities
- Railway network
- 01-Arterial road
- 05-State highway
- 06-National highway-42
- Ward boundary
- Municipal boundary

0 0.5 1 1.5 2 km
1:50,000

Waste service providers

With the appointment of Pratyush, there is a stark divide between public sector-led street sweeping, collection, and recycling, and private businesses in waste picking and trading. This divide is not well reflected in the WasteAware indicators for provider inclusivity (rated 'medium' overall) because Pratyush is well integrated with the municipality, but private and informal pickers and traders are almost entirely excluded.

The waste business in Dhenkanal involves a wide age range, with service providers evenly split between those aged under and over 35 years. There is a clear gender divide, however. Waste trading is highly male dominated, while collectors employed by Pratyush are all women. Waste picking and sweeping includes both men and women.

Table 5.1 Waste workers employed by the municipality and its private sector partner

Municipal personnel		Pratyush personnel	
Role	No.	Role	No.
Sanitation section officer Manages implementation of SWM on the ground	1	**Manager** Overall management on behalf of Pratyush	1
Supervisors Supervising work of sweepers, drivers, and other staff working on SWM. Each supervisor looks after 1 or 2 wards.	12	**Supervisors** Supervising work of waste collectors and sweepers (6) and of operations at MCC and MRF centres (5)	11
Drivers of tractors, JCB, drain ditcher	10	**Drivers** of 8 tractors, 1 JCB, and 1 drain ditcher	10
		Tractor labourers 4 each per tractor	32
Sweepers working in 8 wards	60+	**Sweepers** working in 15 wards, 5 per ward	75
		Extra sweepers miscellaneous work	45
Workers at MCC/MRF	11	**Collectors** 2 per ward in 23 wards	46
Swachh Saathis employed to segregate waste at MCC/MRF centres	25		
Total	119	Total	220

Waste collectors and street sweepers

Pratyush employs 46 people as door-to-door waste collectors. These are almost all women, identified and employed from women's self-help groups. They were the best educated of all the service providers, with four out of six having secondary or higher-secondary-level education. They had received training in driving and how to collect the waste. The street sweepers we interviewed worked for the municipality. None had even a primary level of education and had worked as sweepers for at least 12 years.

Twenty-five *Swachh Saathis*, meaning 'cleanliness friends', are also engaged in the city, selected from women self-help groups. The *Swachh Saathis* played a key role in spreading awareness about segregating waste and paying user fees. The women also work at the composting centres for three to four hours per day, earning Rp 4,000 per month.

None of the waste pickers had been to school or had any relationship with the local authority

Waste pickers

We interviewed three men and two women waste pickers. All had been involved for between 12 and 19 years with some having started in this work as children. None had even a primary level of education. None of the pickers had any relationship with the local authority, were not formally registered (there is no process for that), nor did they belong to an association.

The pickers work in residential neighourhoods. The waste trader we interviewed said his pickers find waste in neighbourhood dumps and buy it from households. The pickers report that municipal waste collection is hampering their ability to grow. This is despite waste volumes in the town growing as the population expands. The most popular and valuable types of waste were plastics, glass, and metal. Most said they sold these to single buyers; only one sold to multiple buyers.

Waste traders

Trading is a male-dominated business, and the men we interviewed had worked in the trade for between 10 and 20 years. As with the pickers, none had education even up to primary level. One worked alone, but the other four employed staff: mostly fewer than five, but one had a workforce larger than this. As with the waste pickers, this business operates informally. None of the businesses is registered, and none has a relationship with the local authority. One of the larger traders estimated there are at least 10 other medium–large businesses operating in the town and another 20 or more smaller businesses. Although they do not have a formal association, they know each other and sometimes work together to sell waste collectively to big players, giving them greater bargaining power over the price.

Despite the increased role of the municipality, the traders all reported that their businesses were expanding as a result of a growing population in the town, and increased customer needs for service. As with the pickers, they trade in plastics, glass, and metal, and also paper and cardboard.

We interviewed one of the larger waste traders, who works with 12 pickers, providing them with bicycle rickshaws and buying all the recyclable waste they collect on a daily basis. His estimates of the volumes he buys suggest that alone he is handling 8 per cent of the paper and cardboard, 9 per cent of the glass, and 2 per cent of the dense plastics generated in the city. The greatest weight of recyclables is in iron and tin. Our household waste quantities and composition assessment did not record high volumes of metals, but larger items may come from businesses or from households but irregularly. Metals for recycling are probably handled entirely by waste traders rather than the municipality.

Waste traders deal in plastics, glass, metal, paper, and cardboard

Table 5.2 Waste quantities handled by one medium–large waste trader in Dhenkanal

	kg/day bought from waste pickers by trader	kg/day generated in the city	Portion of household waste handled by a single trader
Paper	120		
Cartons	200	3187	8%
Plastic	120	6381	2%
Tin	40		
Iron	240	471	59%
Glass	120	1378	9%
Total	840		

Note: We calculated generation rates for the city based on household-generated waste plus 30% for businesses and institutions. It is likely that our assessment under-estimated the quantities of metal waste in the town.

Composting and recycling centres

The municipality has constructed five composting and material recovery centres. Comprehensive data on volumes of waste received for February 2021 showed these centres received on average 1.03 tonnes of organic ('wet') waste and 0.15 tonnes of 'dry' waste. Volumes of wet waste recorded in May and June were higher at 3.3 and 3.1 tonnes per day. This suggests that up to 19 per cent of household organic waste is reaching the centres, and only about 2 per cent of dry waste. For recyclables, this was less than was achieved by a single trader.

Working conditions for waste service providers

The working conditions for all service providers could be improved. All the pickers, traders, and sweepers mentioned problems with occupational diseases, accidents, or other health issues, combined with a lack of PPE. They also all mentioned the lack of access to water, toilets, or handwashing facilities. Only one of the collectors reported wearing gloves, mask, and uniform. Sweepers, on the other hand, were provided with masks and gloves.

All the women waste collectors said they are harassed by the community. Traders and sweepers, on the other hand, say they operate without facing any harassment. Four out of five waste pickers say they face harassment from the community. Survey respondents seemed ambivalent about waste pickers, with 98 per cent saying 'I don't mind them. They are just trying to make a living'.

> **Box 5.1 Case study:**
> **Papun, former waste picker turned successful trader**
>
> I started waste picking at the age of 10 along with my cousins, walking through the lanes of the city to collect waste ... How can I forget those days when I had to bear the beating of the policeman, face the fanatic behaviour of common people, and hold the cheating of *kawadi* (waste) shop owners inside my heart and mind? The police would suspect us of stealing. Older waste pickers would forcefully take our more valuable waste. I slowly learned which locations and times were best for larger quantities of the most valuable waste.
>
> When I was 14, I met Ramesh uncle in the tea shop where I used to go after work. He had just started his own *kawadi* trading business. He inspired me, took me on in his business and three years later, I managed to start my own business. It has taken 10 years to grow to a full-scale business.
>
> The municipality is collecting and managing waste in a better way now ... but they still have a lot to do to make the city 100 per cent clean. I am disappointed, though. We (traders) make the city cleaner and contribute to the solid waste management in the city. However, our effort is not recognized by the municipality.

Governance and regulation

The WasteAware indicators provide an overview of how well the city is performing (Figure 5.6). The municipality has significantly increased its investments in solid waste management and brought in a private sector partner. This has required significant planning, investments, and technical competence. It budgets separately for SWM and since August 2019, charges households a user fee (or 'holding tax'), currently being recovered from 9,430 households (57 per cent). The municipality also receives some income

Up to 19% of household organic waste and 2% of dry waste reaches municipal recycling centres from the composting and material recovery centres of about INR 476,000 per year (US$6,400). From this, it pays for its own staff, vehicles, waste bins, and an awareness programme, and it pays Pratyush for their role.

The municipality invested INR 35.1 m (US$474,000) to construct five recycling centres: four for both composting and material recovery, and one for composting only. The municipality plans to add more centres in future. It used funds partly from its own resources and partly from state funds. The municipality therefore scores medium-high for financial sustainability (5F). The recycling and composting centres are well run, but the municipality as a whole only scores medium for environmental protection (2E) because of how waste is still handled by informal waste pickers and traders and the poorer controls around final disposal.

User inclusivity in planning is also quite good (4U). The SWM drive of the municipality included ward-level meetings where residents had the opportunity to input to the design of the service. The municipality is rated medium in terms of institutional coherence (6L), which includes its ability to plan, supervise, and regulate waste management services. For a municipality of this size, this is a good score.

> To make the SWM efforts successful a sustainable financial model was needed urgently. We conducted a study to understand the 'willingness to pay' by the households. Side by side we undertook a massive awareness and campaigning drive through multiple ways. The campaign ran for six months and focused on household SWM issues, problems, and prospects.
>
> *Executive Officer, Dhenkanal municipality*

Conclusion

Dhenkanal has made remarkable progress in turning around its solid waste management services in a short space of time, and sustained this despite the COVID-19 pandemic. The municipality has set its sights on winning a *Swacha Sarveykhyan* award for the cleanest town. Its approach has sought to invest for 'waste to wealth' rather than simply 'collect and dump'. It is providing a collection service which is valued by residents, and has aimed to divert the majority of waste away from landfill through its decentralized micro-composting and recycling centres. Some waste remains on the streets, but this has decreased significantly, and a good proportion of organic waste is being composted. There is still work to do to change some of the attitudes and behaviours of residents who are not separating waste for the collectors, and who are accepting of littering on the streets.

All this has been carried out, however, in isolation from an existing, vibrant set of waste pickers and traders. These businesses continue to process significant quantities of valuable waste, handling more of the dry recyclables than achieved by the municipality. They have developed knowledge and relationships over many years which give them huge expertise in sorting, categorizing, and bulking waste in ways that are required by recycling industries. Some of the poorest people in the town earn a living as pickers supplying these traders. The municipality's vision for SWM in the town does not include these businesses and although its full effect may not yet be seen, over time the collection efforts of the municipality may undermine the viability of these informal businesses.

The municipality invested US$474,000 to construct five recycling centres

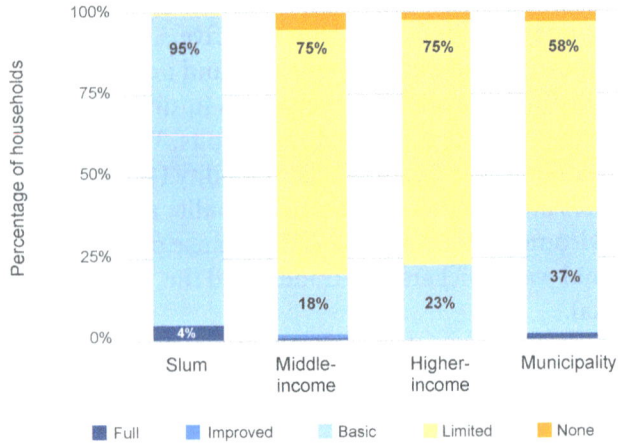

Figure 5.3 Waste services ladder by wealth category

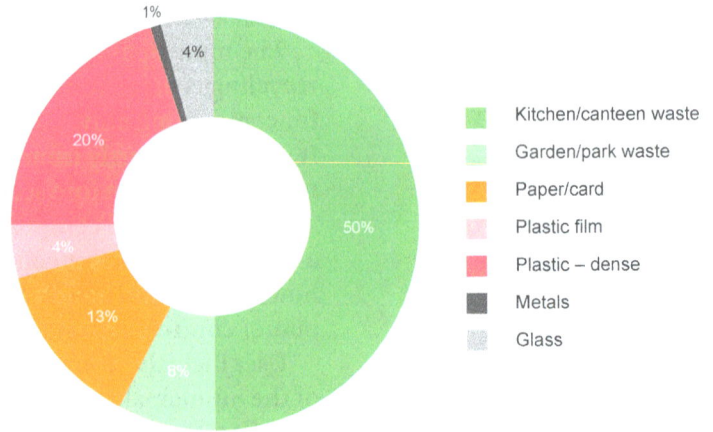

Full Improved Basic Limited None

Kitchen/canteen waste
Garden/park waste
Paper/card
Plastic film
Plastic – dense
Metals
Glass

Figure 5.4 Composition of household waste, whole municipality

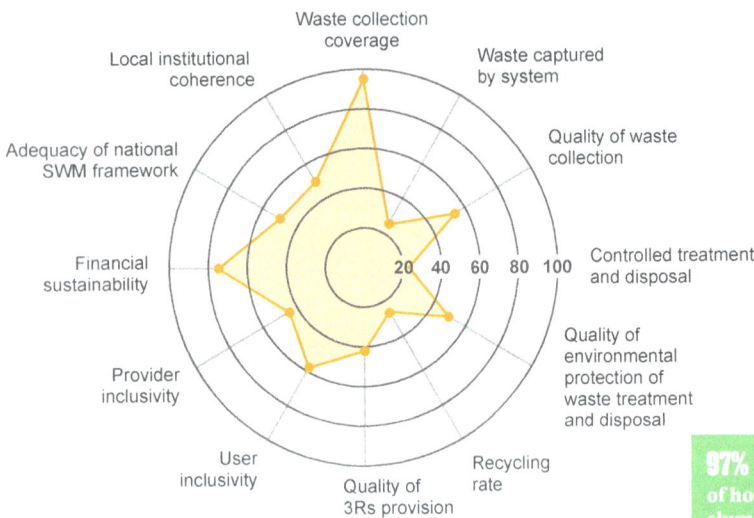

Figure 5.6 WasteAware indicators

0.24 KG Slums   **0.30 KG** Middle income   **0.43 KG** Higher income   **0.33 KG** Average for whole town

Figure 5.5 Average weight of waste per person per day

97% of households including slum communities have their waste collected regularly and reliably

POOR ATTITUDES to littering remain despite recent awareness campaigns

41% of dry recyclable waste collected and sold by informal waste sector, but only 3% through municipal services

Figure 5.7 Municipal waste flows

Key:

🛆 Tonnes per day

● Private service providers

● Municipal/public services

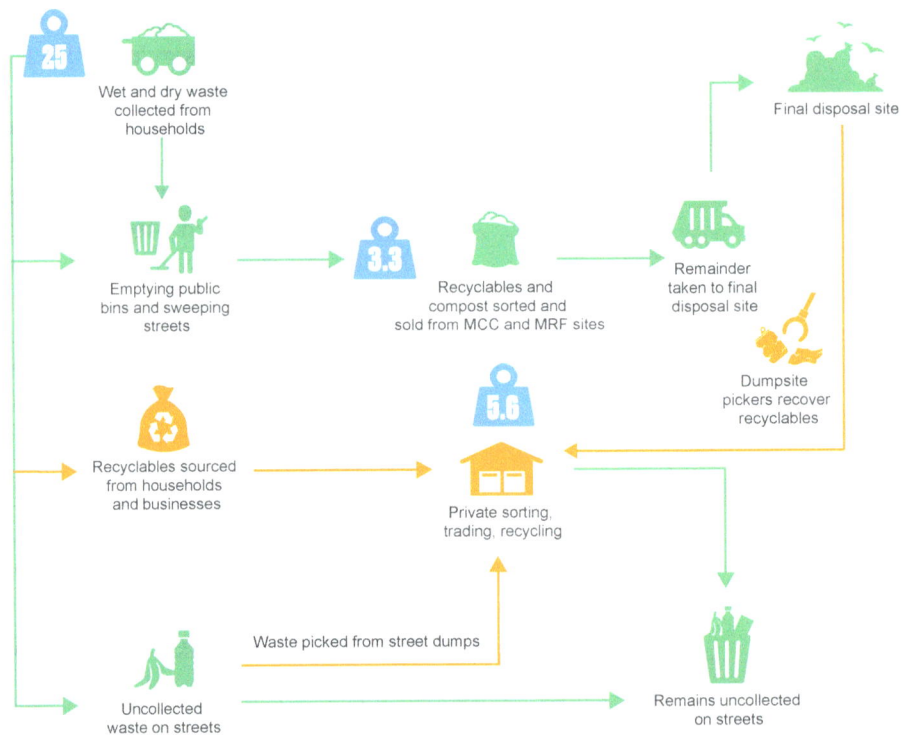

While service rates suggest that 25 tonnes per day is collected, this does not match with the records of waste received at MRF and MCC sites. We were not able to establish a clear explanation for this.

6 KISUMU, KENYA

Kenya's urban population is large and continues to grow, increasing by 2.3 million (19 per cent) between the 2009 and 2019 censuses. Around 14.8 million Kenyans (31 per cent) live in urban areas. While this is concentrated in the largest cities (42 per cent in Nairobi, Mombasa, and Nakuru), the numbers of towns with populations between 100,000 and 1 million has grown from just 4 in 1999 to 22 in 2009.[1] With it, the amount of solid waste generated continues to grow rapidly. The government estimates that by 2030, Kenya will generate three times more municipal waste than in 2009 (MoEF, 2021).

Until recently, actions on municipal waste management were guided by the National Environment Policy (2014) and Waste Management Strategy (2015). These policies focus on reducing pollution and risks from hazardous waste, giving little direction on waste minimization and recycling, and seeing waste as a problem not a resource. However, the draft National Sustainable Waste Management Policy (MoEF, 2021) recognizes these shortcomings and shifts its emphasis to prioritizing waste minimization and a circular economy. There is scope for support from climate change policies, as Kenya's national commitments to the Paris Agreement included actions for sustainable waste management systems (MoENR, 2015). A NAMA action plan for Nairobi estimates it could save 0.8 million tCO_2e per year (MoENR, 2017).

Since 2010, responsibility for solid waste management lies with county governments in Kenya's devolved system. It takes time for each county to localize national policy changes in their own legislation and targets.

Kisumu City: background and waste management structures

Kisumu is Kenya's third largest urban centre. The county's population in 2019 was 1.16 million (KNBS, 2019). The city operates as a semi-autonomous body under the county government, with a population of 501,818.[2] The 2019 census gives Kisumu City's urban population as 398,000, as even within the city boundary not all residents are considered 'urban'. However, we use the number within the wards governed by the city for our estimates. For our surveys, we selected four contrasting settlements. The higher-middle–income estate of Tom Mboya, middle-income Migosi, and low-income Manyatta B and Nyalenda A.

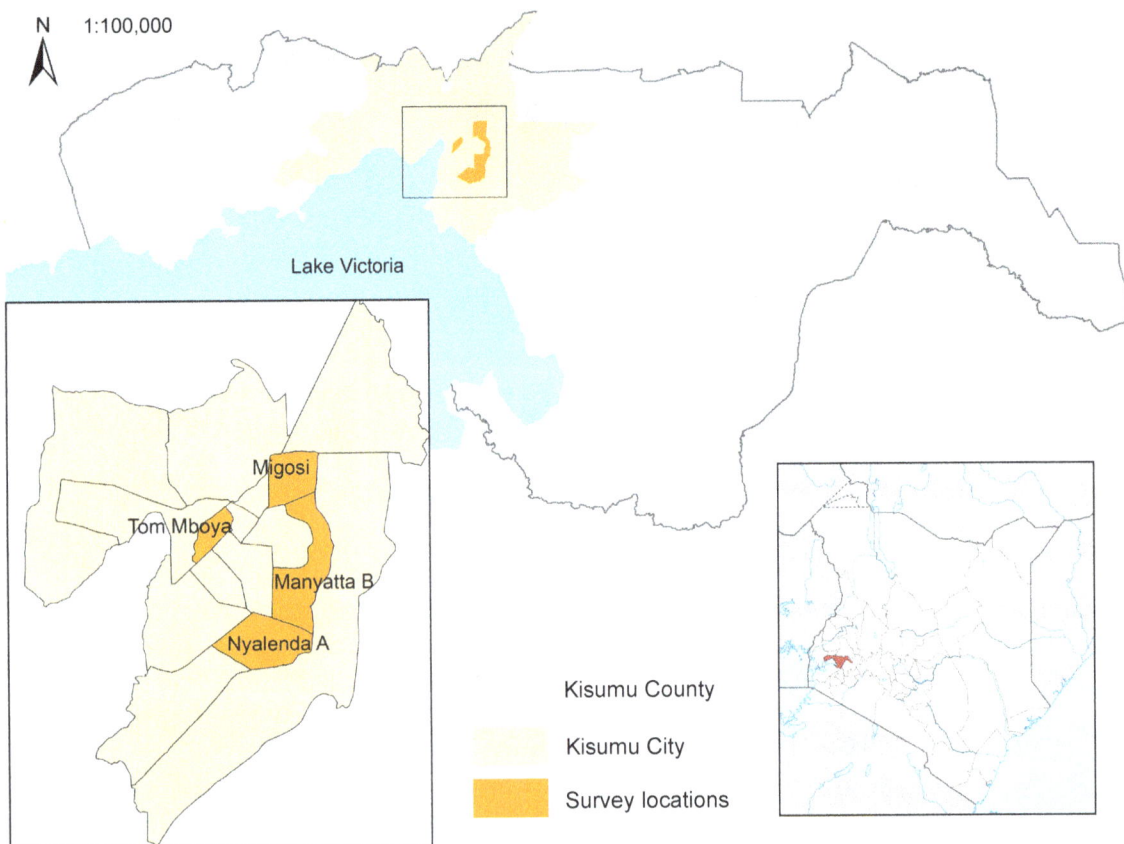

Figure 6.1 Kisumu County and Kisumu City, with survey locations

The city serves as a commercial and transport hub for the western part of Kenya, with a large part of the county's population engaged in trade, fishing, and farming. The county government estimates 60 per cent of the workforce are in the informal sector (Kisumu County, 2018). Levels of poverty are high, with 40 per cent below the national poverty line in 2016 (KNBS, 2017). Around 60 per cent live in 'low-income settlements',[3] many of which suffer from a high water table and seasonal flooding. Climate scenarios predict greater extremes with several months being wetter on average, and others drier in the future (Bahadur and Dodman, 2021).

Kisumu County developed its Solid Waste Management Act in 2015 and a comprehensive Kisumu Integrated Solid Waste Management Plan (KISWaMP) for 2015–2025, updated in 2017 (Kisumu County, 2017). This followed an earlier poorly implemented strategy (2010). The strategy's first two key areas for action are on waste reduction, and recycling and composting (rather than collection and dumping). This is further supported by a 2020 Kisumu County SWM Policy and Bill.

This ambition is not well matched with resources. A Deputy Director of Environment manages three superintendents responsible for the central business district, commercial areas (bus parks and markets), and residential areas. There is a team of four drivers, 15 loaders, 12 sweepers, and 166 casual staff. In most residential areas, all that is possible is removing waste after occasional clean-up activities. A variety of private companies (formal and informal) provide patchy access to collection services.

The Department of Environment is also responsible for the Kachok open dumpsite, located less than 2 km from the central business district and in use since 1975. Efforts were made to decommission the site in 2017, removing waste to a site further away from the city, as a key electoral pledge of a newly elected County Governor. However, this stalled and disposal at Kachok resumed in 2018 (Awuor et al., 2019). The level of environmental controls is very poor ('low' for WasteAware 2E, see Figure 6.7). Waste is dumped and compacted without record keeping. A tipping fee used to be charged, but this was abolished when private operators complained of poor quality service at the site.

Household access to waste services

The city's waste services only reach residential areas in minimal ways, clearing litter from open spaces. The city does not provide formal disposal points. Access to household waste services, therefore, relies on private providers (formal and informal) and community action. Our waste ladder considers four key elements of service provision:

1. *Access:* In residential areas, access to a waste service depends on whether private operators exist in an area, and whether households are willing to pay for their services. Weighting our findings across the whole city, we found 29 per cent of households use collection services and 65 per cent have no access to a waste service.[4] In richer areas, services are procured by estate management companies. Landlords sometimes play a role in low-income areas, for example arranging for private operators to remove waste from a communal disposal point (accessed by 14 per cent of households in Manyatta).

   Households adopt a number of strategies to manage their waste, separating it for disposal in different places depending on how flammable, hazardous, or unpleasant it is. A lot of waste is burned as a way of 'getting rid' of it, and some is saved to help start cooking fires. The rest is thrown onto open ground (Figure 6.2). Some waste is thrown into pit latrines, in particular in Nyalenda A (70 per cent of households) and Manyatta B (63 per cent), especially menstrual waste, nappies, and medical waste. Neighbourhood clean-ups are relatively common. However, sometimes the heaps of waste are not removed, so it is not long before it spreads out again.

2. *Quality:* Collection services are generally weekly, and operate reliably, and 95 per cent with a collection service say waste is collected as scheduled 'most' or 'almost all' of the time. Of those using communal disposal points, only around half were happy with their

A variety of private companies provide patchy access to collection services

65% of households have no access to a waste service

In Nyalenda A, 70% of households throw waste into pit latrines

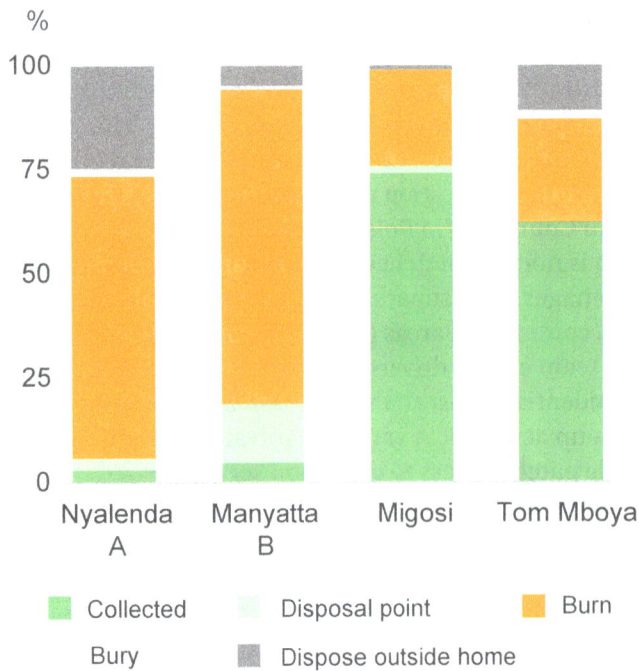

Figure 6.2 How households in Kisumu deal with the bulk of their waste

management, with others saying they were dirty, poorly managed, or hazardous.

3. *Impact*: Despite the lack of services, households tended not to rate the 'impact of indiscriminate waste dumping in our area' as severe (only 50 per cent in Nyalenda A and 34 per cent in Manyatta B). Some said they were just 'used to it' and other problems were a bigger concern. However, the impact was at least 'moderate' for three-quarters of residents in all neighbourhoods except higher-income Tom Mboya. Impacts were rated as equally severe by both men and women.

4. *Separation for recycling*: Waste separation for recycling or reuse is limited. Citywide, only 21 per cent of households separate waste for recycling. This is only 7 per cent in Manyatta B and Tom Mboya, rising to 30 per cent in Nyalenda A. The variation seems to depend on whether collectors visit door-to-door for recyclables in a particular area. Plastics were the most commonly separated, followed by glass, metals, paper and cardboard, and organics.

The combined waste ladder (see Figure 6.4 at the end of the chapter) illustrates huge citywide inequalities in service, with low-income households having no or limited services, while over half have at least basic services in middle-income areas, and improved services in richer neighbourhoods.

Elaborating on the impacts of poor waste management, the top three problems from our survey were the smell, flies, and mosquitoes. Women from Nyalenda and Manyatta also highlighted how waste was a hazard for children. Blocked drainage was mentioned, but not as frequently as other issues. The problems were most acute during the rainy season.

A concern highlighted in all the focus groups was the River Auji which runs through the settlements. The river is used for dumping waste, and carries waste from upstream settlements. Participants said it carries 'everything that can be called waste … plastic, organics, sanitary pads, human waste, dead animals, aborted infants, dead bodies …'. The area is

Citywide, only 21% of households separate waste for recycling

The river is
a particular
hotspot, but
waste problems
are evident
throughout the
neighbourhoods

'pathetic, a disaster because sometimes children bathe and fish there, water is used for washing ...'. The people who live along the river 'suffer a lot ... It causes the presence of rodents, flies, mosquitoes, and foul smell'. When the river floods, waste spreads out to the surrounding compounds and into people's houses.[5] The river is a particular hotspot, but the maps drawn in focus groups and hotspot analysis by enumerators showed waste problems throughout the neighbourhoods, on open ground, by markets, and near large groups of houses and businesses, all causing 'flies, mosquitoes and foul smells' (Figure 6.3).

Responsibilities for waste management are gendered. Focus group participants confirmed that it is usually women who manage waste, and who pay for waste services. The caretaker of one plot explained she had to work hard to persuade tenants to sort waste so that food scraps would feed her poultry, recyclables given to waste pickers, and the remainder burned, 'but still some tenants are a constant bother since they do not observe the rules ... It's a collective effort ...'.

Coping strategies to deal with waste in the absence of effective services include burning waste. Residents in Nyalenda explained how a slight depression in the land is used as a dump and waste is burned there. But the waste does not burn well during the rainy season, the area fills with water and the waste spreads. Around a quarter of residents in Nyalenda and Manyatta said they struggle to dispose in particular of menstrual pads (28 per cent) and nappies (25 per cent).

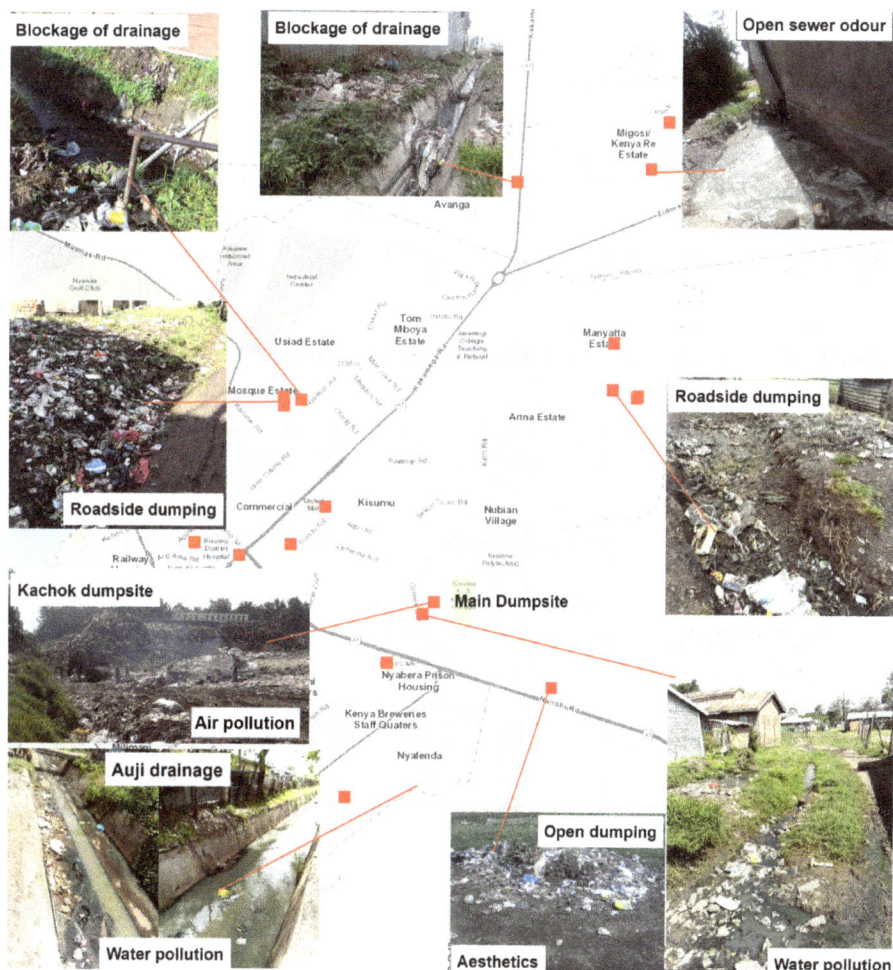

Figure 6.3 Negative impacts of waste in Kisumu

Household waste composition

We found that 61 per cent of the city's household waste is organic. Despite the plastic bag ban, 3 per cent of waste is thin film plastic, and another 4 per cent dense plastic. Also, 11 per cent of waste (by weight) was nappies and sanitary pads with a greater weight found in middle- and higher-income neighbourhoods (Figure 6.5).[6] The National Environment Management Authority (NEMA) director noted that these products made up a large portion of waste collected during a recent lakeshore clean-up.

The COVID-19 pandemic caused some changes in waste. Two-thirds of service providers said waste had increased, and others found valuable recyclables were less available due to the collapse of the town's hospitality trade.

Waste service providers

City officials say there are at least 700 people working in waste management in Kisumu, with conservative estimates of 200 people in private formal enterprises and of 300 working informally, in addition to 197 employed by the county. Together they help to deal with approximately 252 tonnes of waste generated every day, with each resident generating on average 0.39 kg per day (Figure 6.6).[7]

Recently, the waste business has attracted new entrants, particularly collectors. Of the 21 service providers we interviewed, 12 (57 per cent) had been involved for three years or less. Others (eight), particularly waste pickers, had been involved for far longer (10 years or more). Irrespective of length of service, the waste sector in Kisumu is youth-dominated and male-dominated. Two-thirds of those we interviewed were under 35. Most roles are done by men with only sorting and some types of value-addition having a more equal gender balance.

There is a range in the formality of businesses. Just under half were registered with business licences, and four had environmental licences (which service providers said were prohibitively expensive). Waste traders, although well established, were the least likely to be formally licensed. The county and regulator have focused on collectors rather than recycling businesses in terms of controls and recognition. Only six service providers (28 per cent) had received training. Three (of 21) were members of a waste association: the Kisumu Waste Management Association (KIWAN), which has a membership of 27 organizations employing 85 people.

Waste pickers or 'scavengers'

About 70 waste pickers or 'scavengers' operate at Kachok dumpsite, and more work in residential areas. They select the most valuable types of waste: metals, plastics, and paper, and sell to traders. Pickers have operated in Kisumu for a long time (Box 6.2). Others have joined more recently: 'before, people were afraid of waste picking, but now many people have come into the business' increasing competition. Some also commented that access to valuable waste has reduced as more traders are going directly to households and businesses for separated waste, squeezing out the pickers.

The Kachok dumpsite has been the focus of considerable political attention, as well as research. A pickers' leader said 'when people with cameras come here, guys do not want to talk ... because so many have come and made empty promises. They use us as ladders to their own success'. The pickers agree who picks which types of waste, and who has first access to particular trucks. They control who can pick waste at the dumpsite.

About 252 tonnes of waste is generated every day in Kisumu

Two-thirds of waste service providers were under 35

> **Box 6.1 Case study: Winnie Auma, waste picker in Manyatta**
>
> Winnie started as a waste picker about five years ago after struggling to make ends meet. A friend showed her which materials were valuable. 'I did not need any capital to start. I could walk around and pick up the recyclable waste from the ground and after functions... Then I started asking door-to-door'. She says 'I face discrimination as a woman in this business...' She can't start as early as some because as a wife and mother she has to first take care of the children, husband, and family chores. She often suffers cuts and other injuries, but tries not to spend money on medical treatment. Overall, 'I have made many positive strides in my life ever since I started in this business'.

> **Box 6.2 Case study: Jackson Omondi Okuro,**
> **waste picker and leader at Kachok dumpsite**
>
> Jackson started picking waste as a child in 2012 after dropping out of school in form 3. 'I could see how [my father] managed to take care of the family with the income he got from here'. He started partly to avoid getting mixed up in crime. It takes skill to quickly pick out valuable materials. 'I have managed to find other jobs from time to time, but when I compare the income, I always return here'.
>
> To work here, you must be *roho juu* (courageous), and be ready to be called names. Sometimes criminals come here with stolen goods, and 'everybody gets caught in the mess when the law enforcers come calling'.
>
> 'This is my life and I do not see any other future ... but if I work hard and focus, I can provide [for my family] as a man should'.

In our survey, there was ambivalence about waste pickers. Citywide, around half (55 per cent) said 'I don't mind them. They are just trying to make a living'. Just over a quarter (27 per cent) said they are doing a good job (particularly in Migosi and Nyalenda). In better-off Tom Mboya, however, half (51 per cent) see waste pickers as a nuisance.

Waste collectors

53 tonnes of waste per day is collected from households

Waste collecting has flourished since the county government authorized private collection services, collecting an estimated 53 tonnes per day from households. Most are small-scale, collecting from 20–50 households. They often try to balance low- and high-income clients. For example, Libeto Youth Group serves 10 clients in upmarket Milimani, and 40 in Nyalenda. Customer willingness and ability to pay was a challenge hindering business growth for three out five. In Nyalenda, Libeto allows two households to share a collection bag, halving the cost between them.

These businesses do not expect households to separate waste, picking out valuables later to sell to traders. They take the remainder to a local dumping ground, or if they are close enough, to Kachok.

Waste traders

There are thriving waste trading businesses in Kisumu, aggregating recyclables and selling to processors mostly in Nairobi. They generally buy from pickers and collect separated waste directly from households and businesses. The sector is expanding. Traders said their businesses were growing and four out of five had started their business three years ago or more recently. The traders all employ staff: some with up to five and others with more than 20 staff.

All the traders aggregate metals and four also work with plastics. They all had multiple but reliable buyers. One of the more established enterprises purchased about 2 tonnes per day. Seven such enterprises are members of KIWAN, potentially handling around 14 tonnes per day. The business can be difficult because prices fluctuate and cash flow can be a problem. They need opportunities to invest in additional storage space and recycling equipment.

Street sweepers: government and private sector

The City Department of Environment employs staff who concentrate on sweeping streets and collecting waste from designated disposal points in public areas. Private companies sweep the streets in middle- and higher-income estates. They take the waste to local sites (1-2 km) where much of it is burned, and some valuable items are sold to traders.

Working conditions, harassment, and discrimination

Working conditions for all waste workers are hazardous. Pickers and collectors are exposed to the greatest risks. Among traders, five out of six used PPE, while none of the lone waste pickers did. In the focus groups and surveys, injuries and sickness were seen as the most severe risks. At least half of the pickers, traders, and collectors also noted the lack of access to water, toilets, or handwashing at work. A lack of shade made working conditions hard.

Two-thirds of waste workers, particularly waste pickers (five out of six) said they faced harassment at work. Harassment came from the local community, police, family members, and sometimes the regulator (NEMA). Working as a waste picker can make it difficult to get other jobs, because you become labelled as a gangster or thief. Workers are proud of their contribution though, saying 'this is a decent way to make a living' and it helps the environment.

> **Social assumptions reduce rights of waste pickers**
>
> 'We do not have a voice. Even if someone wrongs you and you complain, you are not taken seriously ... It is seen like it's normal for that to happen because we are "ninjas".'
>
> *Waste picker*

Voluntary community action by CBOs, NGOs, and neighbourhood associations

The county government occasionally clears waste from open spaces in residential areas. In addition, in Nyalenda A and Manyatta B, residents mentioned the *Kazi kwa Vijana* (Work for Youth) initiative, or the COVID-related *Kazi Mtaani* which worked to clear waste, sometimes daily or weekly.

These provide casual employment and skills training for youth in labour-intensive activities. Sometimes, this was not then removed to the dumpsite, causing more problems. However, residents were positive, 'if *Kazi Mtaani* can continue then my neighbourhood will forever be clean and safe, so I want it to be there permanently, creating employment for youth'. Overall, there was good awareness about littering with 90 per cent saying, 'it's bad. We should all take responsibility'.

Governance and regulation

The WasteAware indicators provide an overview of how well the city is performing (Figure 6.7). Waste management services in Kisumu's residential areas have been left to the market. There are active, committed service providers making a difference in both low-income and better-off areas in collection and recycling. However, there is almost no engagement with service providers. KIWAN is keen to engage and feel they have a lot to offer. Equally there is limited capacity for effective engagement with users. The city scores 'low-medium' for provider and 'low' for user inclusivity.

We have noted that current policies and strategies are shifting the emphasis from regulation of collectors to more active promotion of waste reduction and recycling. However, the capacity to implement these strategies, or make sure service provision is equitable, is very limited (as noted in the KISWaMP strategy). There is limited staffing, and few functional vehicles: three 2-tonne trucks, six farm tractors, 12 trailers, one skip loader (broken down), and one pick-up truck. None of these is specifically designed to carry waste, but at least they are relatively easy to maintain. There is a financial allocation of KSh 100 m for annual recurrent costs of running trucks and paying workers, which is not adequate to cover needs. The city scores low-medium for financial sustainability (5F) and local institutional coherence (6L).

The city's capacity to implement waste reduction and recycling strategies is very limited

Conclusion

The waste management system in Kisumu still leaves much to be desired. Access to household waste services depends on whether a service provider operates in a neighbourhood and whether a household is willing to pay. The impacts on the living environment are severe, with knock-on effects on health and flood risks. The capacity (leadership, equipment, staffing, and budgets) of the City Department of Environment is extremely limited compared to the scale of the task.

There are positive elements of the waste management system in Kisumu which, if harnessed, could be the building blocks for significant improvements. Recent policies and strategies emphasize waste minimization and recycling. Vibrant and growing private operators, both formal and informal, mean there is expertise to be tapped. The work of *Kazi Mtaani* was generally welcomed.

Political focus in Kisumu has centred on the Kachok dumpsite. City managers are placing hope in a proposed landfill 25 km away as a key to solving the city's waste crisis. However, the distance adds costs and time to already limited operational budgets. To make effective use of a new landfill, the waste system itself needs to be reoriented, with only residual, non-recyclable waste taken there. This would require far greater emphasis on source separation, full cooperation with existing pickers, collectors, and waste traders, and new initiatives to promote area-wide coverage in collection services.

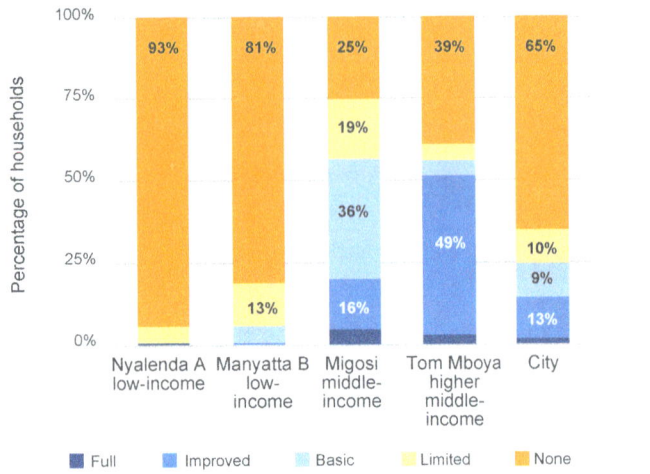

Figure 6.4 Waste services ladder by wealth category

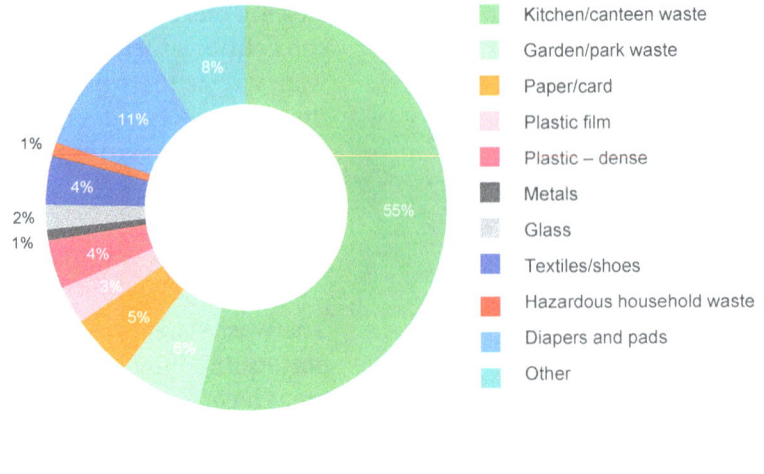

Percentage of households

Nyalenda A low-income: None 93%, Limited, Basic, Improved, Full
Manyatta B low-income: None 81%, Limited 13%
Migosi middle-income: None 25%, Limited 19%, Basic 36%, Improved 16%
Tom Mboya higher middle-income: None 39%, Improved 49%
City: None 65%, Limited 10%, Basic 9%, Improved 13%

Key: Full, Improved, Basic, Limited, None

Figure 6.5 Composition of household waste, whole city

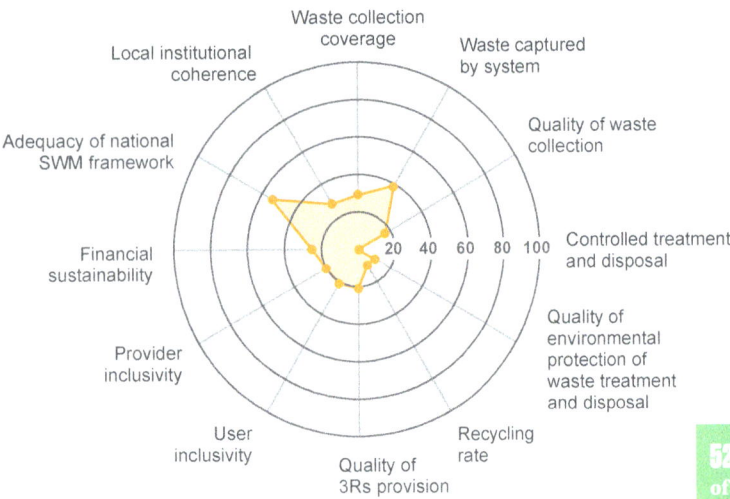

- Kitchen/canteen waste — 55%
- Garden/park waste
- Paper/card — 5%
- Plastic film — 3%
- Plastic – dense — 4%
- Metals — 1%
- Glass — 2%
- Textiles/shoes — 4%, 11%
- Hazardous household waste — 1%
- Diapers and pads
- Other — 8%

Figure 6.7 WasteAware indicators

Waste collection coverage, Waste captured by system, Quality of waste collection, Controlled treatment and disposal, Quality of environmental protection of waste treatment and disposal, Recycling rate, Quality of 3Rs provision, User inclusivity, Provider inclusivity, Financial sustainability, Adequacy of national SWM framework, Local institutional coherence

Figure 6.6 Average weight of waste per person per day

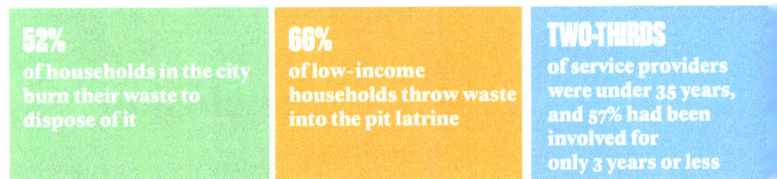

0.35 KG — Slums
0.46 KG — Middle income
0.47 KG — Higher income
0.39 KG — Average for whole city

52% of households in the city burn their waste to dispose of it

66% of low-income households throw waste into the pit latrine

TWO-THIRDS of service providers were under 35 years, and 57% had been involved for only 3 years or less

Figure 6.8 Municipal waste flows

Key:
- Tonnes per day
- Private service providers
- Municipal/public services

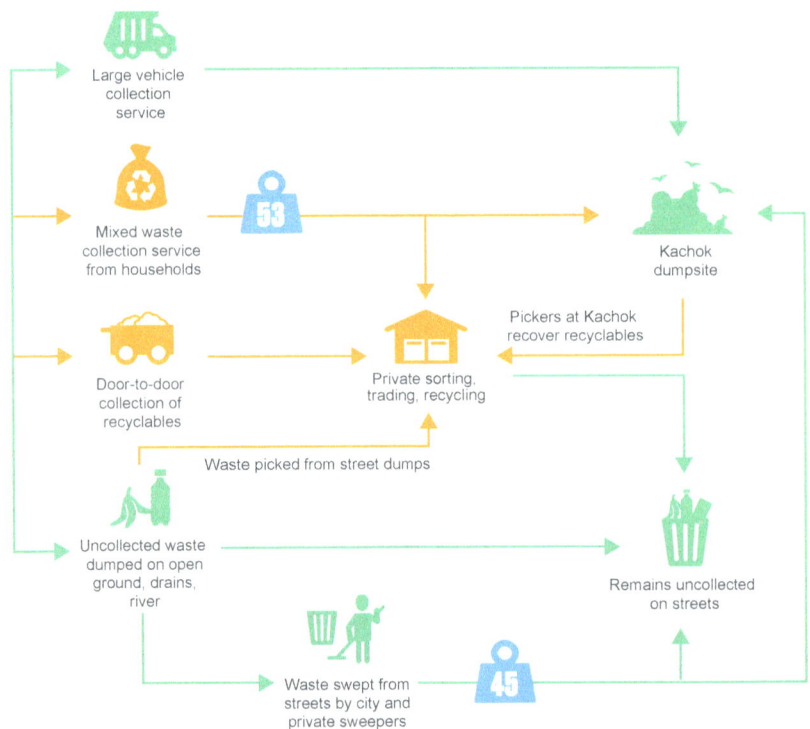

WASTE GENERATORS — 252

Large vehicle collection service
Mixed waste collection service from households — 53
Door-to-door collection of recyclables
Private sorting, trading, recycling
Kachok dumpsite
Pickers at Kachok recover recyclables
Waste picked from street dumps
Uncollected waste dumped on open ground, drains, river
Remains uncollected on streets
Waste swept from streets by city and private sweepers — 45

7 DAKAR, SENEGAL

Senegal is the westernmost country in mainland Africa, with a population of around 16 million. The majority of the population lives on the coast and works in agriculture or other food industries. The rapid urban population growth (3.7 per cent in 2019; see World Bank, 2018a) makes solid waste management a key challenge in Senegal and poses serious public health and environmental threats, especially as 30 per cent of the urban population lives in slums (World Bank, 2018b). Its coastal location means Senegal is a large contributor to ocean waste pollution, ranking 21st in the world, only just behind the USA (Jambeck et al., 2015). National generation of municipal solid waste is predicted to more than triple between 2016 and 2050 (Kaza et al., 2018: 207).

Increasing political attention has been focused on the waste management crisis in recent years. A national programme for solid waste management has been established which sets performance and results targets. To try to tackle fragmented responsibilities, a national waste coordinating unit (UCG) was established in 2015 within the Ministry of Local Government. The UCG also took over responsibility for waste management in Dakar and allowed small local private entities to provide collection services, transforming the service in Dakar with daily collections and street cleaning (Kaza et al., 2018). A 'zero waste' programme focusing on plastic waste was launched in 2019 following a national plastic ban in 2016 which was not very successfully implemented. In March 2020, the World Bank also approved US$125 m to support improving waste management. Improving waste management is also seen as a central part of the national 'Plan Sénégal Emergent', a green growth roadmap to meet the SDGs and Paris Agreement commitments.

Dakar: background and waste management

Dakar is Senegal's economic and political capital. Dakar Region is home to around a quarter of the country's population (estimated 3,835,019 people in 2020; see MEFP/ANSD, 2015), 55 per cent of the nation's GDP (World Bank, 2017), and 13 per cent of Senegal's poor (ANSD, 2016). Dakar city (estimated at 2,470,000 in 2020) lies on a narrow, highly urbanized peninsula. Dakar attracts most of the country's industrial, commercial, and financial activities, with a large port for international trade. The population is predominantly young. The middle- to higher-income population lives in Dakar *département*, while lower-income communities tend to live outside the peninsula in the districts (*départements*) of Pikine and Rufisque.

Increasing volumes of municipal waste outpace the authorities' ability to manage it: 2,300 to 2,600 tonnes of waste is generated per day in Dakar *département* alone and each person generates 0.58 kg of solid waste daily.[1] Yearly, this adds up to 750,000 tonnes. Uncollected waste results in blocked rainwater drains (especially near markets) and flooding, as well as toxic gas emissions and pests. Decades of an 'everything must go to landfill' policy have also led to ever increasing quantities of unrecycled waste.

The Mbeubeuss open dumping site was first established in 1968 and now covers an area of 114 hectares. An estimated 1,300 tonnes of waste arrive there every day. Around 2,000 waste pickers operate at the site, recovering items for recycling (Ehui, 2020). However, the dump represents a huge source of environmental pollution.

For this comparative analysis we selected four contrasting settlements across Dakar Region: the higher-middle–income Point E in Dakar and

2,300–2,600 tonnes of waste is generated per day in Dakar

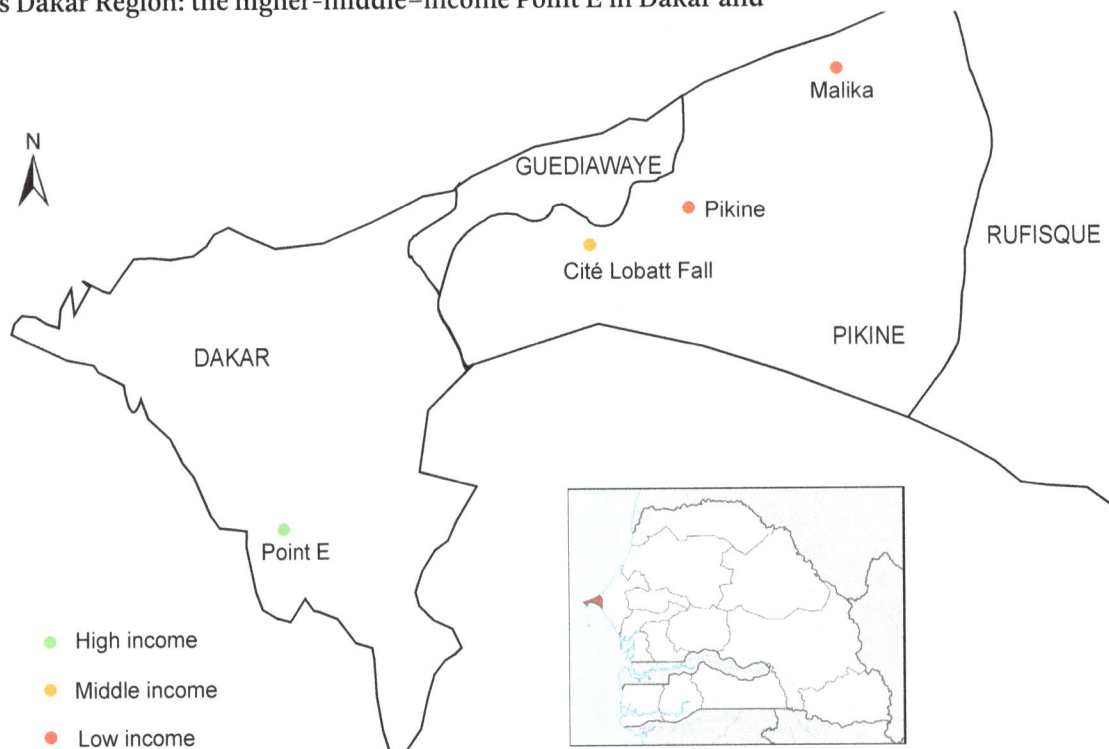

Figure 7.1 Dakar Région map, with the four neighbourhoods selected for the study

Source: adapted from NordNordWest, https://creativecommons.org/licenses/by-sa/4.0/deed.en

middle-income Cité Lobatt Fall, and low-income settlements Pikine and Malika in Pikine (Figure 7.1).[2]

Household access to waste services

Households are happy with waste collection, but indiscriminate disposal remains a big issue

Waste collection services for households are provided by different operators across the city. In higher-income neighbourhoods with easily accessible streets, UCG trucks collect waste directly. In other neighbourhoods, private service providers operate. Households bring waste onto the streets by their houses on an agreed schedule for collection. In most cases the waste is taken to points where it can be transferred in bulk by UCG or other licensed operators to Mbeubeuss. This second stage of transport does not always happen, and causes 'many illegal dumpsites' within or near neighbourhoods (Mberu et al., 2018). So even while households' satisfaction with collection is high, indiscriminate disposal remains a big issue. Estimates vary, but between 30 per cent (WIEGO, 2020) and 50 per cent (Ehui, 2020) of generated waste is collected and taken to the landfill. Our waste ladder considers four key elements of service provision:

1. *Access*: Access to some sort of service (collection or a disposal point) was nearly universal (99 per cent). This compares favourably with other sub-Saharan African cities.[3] In Malika, Point E, and for a quarter of residents in Cité Lobatt Fall, this was a doorstep collection service (36 per cent citywide). In Malika, informal collectors use animal-drawn carts which can navigate sandy, unplanned neigh-bourhoods. In Pikine and for three-quarters in Cité Lobatt Fall, residents bring waste to an agreed disposal point (63 per cent citywide).

2. *Quality*: Collection services operated daily in better-off Point E and Cité Lobatt Fall. In Malika, collections were daily (44 per cent) or two to three times a week (56 per cent), for which residents paid a negotiated fee of CFA 1,000–1,500 (€1.5–3) monthly. Fees could be as high as CFA 5,000 in Cité Lobatt Fall, while in Point E residents pay a communal tax of up to CFA 10,000 (€15). Collection services were reported as reliable, with 98 per cent saying they came as scheduled 'most of the time' or 'almost all of the time'. Informal providers in Malika were rated as marginally less reliable than local government. Irrespective of location or service provider, 96 per cent were satisfied with their collection service.

Figure 7.2 Indiscriminate waste disposal in Dakar

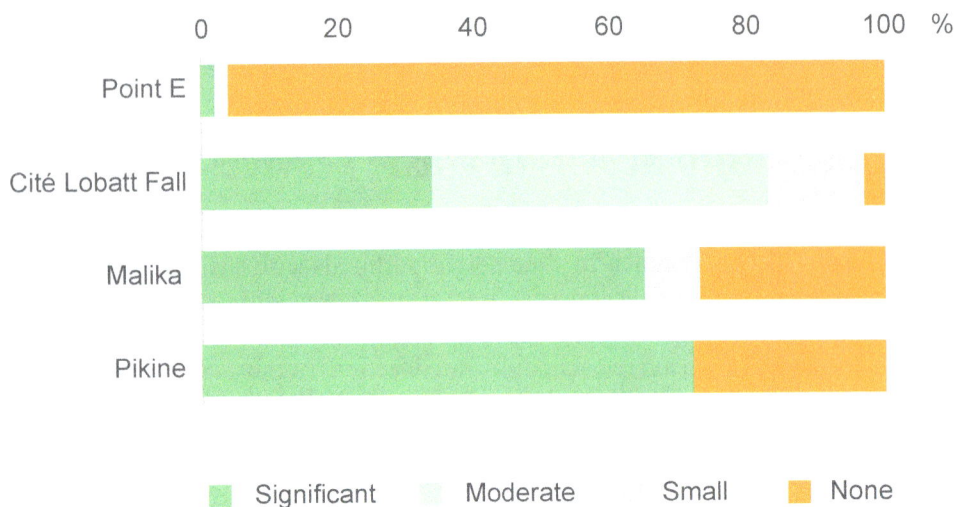

Figure 7.3 showing percentages from 0 to 100%, categories: Point E, Cité Lobatt Fall, Malika, Pikine. Legend: Significant, Moderate, Small, None.

Figure 7.3 Perception of impact of solid waste disposal in the neighbourhood

At the disposal points, waste is cleared daily. The majority (90 per cent) reported these points were clean, well managed, and with waste contained, although some complained that waste piles up where people know the trucks park. The points were not convenient, being more than 200 m away for residents in Pikine, and for 45 per cent of users in Cité Lobatt Fall. Residents complained, saying we 'deplore the distance of the collection point from [our] homes'.

There is a gender divide in managing waste. Focus group participants confirmed that 'women tend to be in charge of disposing waste for households'. Where fees are paid for collection, women also said they are in charge of the subscription.

3. *Impact*: Despite the collection services and disposal points, residents reported that indiscriminate dumping of waste was creating a 'significant' impact in their neighbourhood, especially in low-income neighbourhoods (Figure 7.3). In contrast, only 34 per cent in Cité Lobatt Fall complained of 'significant' impacts. In Point E, 96 per cent said there was 'no impact'.

4. *Separation for recycling*: Waste collectors do not require households to segregate waste. However, specialized waste collectors also visit households. They offer small payments for valuable materials, or simply provide a free service. Comprehensive collection services seem to eliminate these opportunities, so in Point E only 4 per cent of households separate waste at home. In contrast, in Pikine where households have to take waste to a distant disposal point, 72 per cent separate at least one waste type, as do a third (34 per cent) of households in Cité Lobatt Fall. Most only separate one type of waste, with organics being the most common, followed by metals and glass.

The combined waste ladder (Figure 7.6) illustrates huge citywide inequalities in service. Richer Point E has an almost universal 'improved' service. It does not reach 'full' service levels because of the lack of separation for recycling. In other neighbourhoods, high proportions of households still only have 'limited' service because of the impacts waste continues to have in their neighbourhood.

Elaborating on the impacts of waste, hotspot mapping identified examples of illegal dumping in unoccupied plots, open spaces, and along roadsides. This is despite people (88 per cent of those interviewed) agreeing

There are huge citywide inequalities in waste service

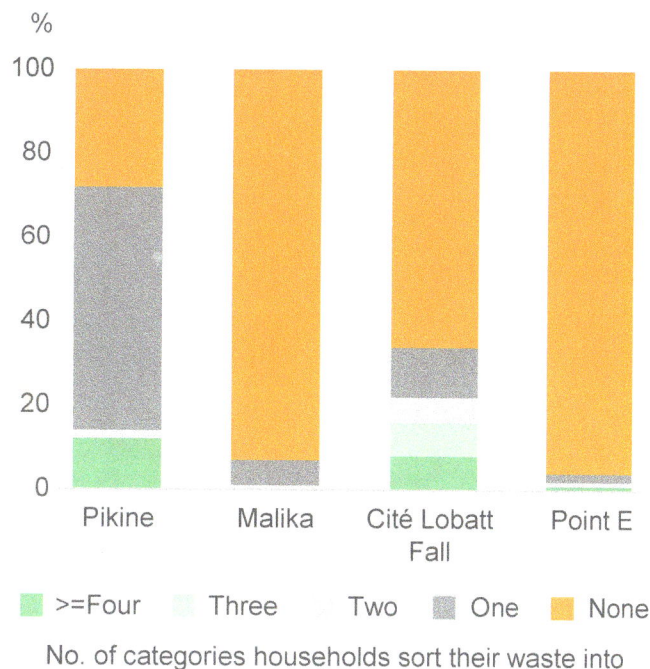

Figure 7.4 Proportion of households separating waste at home

that throwing waste on the street was 'bad: we should all take responsibility for keeping our area clean'. Focus group participants in Pikine described how collectors using animal-drawn carts regularly dispose of the waste in nearby unoccupied plots. Sometimes, this waste is burned to try to control the problems. Households continue to be directly responsible for some waste dumping. In addition to household waste, respondents identified local markets, public transport points, and schools as generating 'the most significant solid waste issues'.

Table 7.1 Types of waste separated by those who segregate at home

Waste type	Households separating	
	No. (of 117)	%
Organics	98	83.8
Metals	36	30.8
Glass	30	25.6
Plastics	28	23.9
Paper/cardboard	17	14.5
Textiles	9	7.7

Leachate flows from the dump into a lake, spreading pollution to vegetable plots

The impacts of this waste included blocked drains, pests such as flies and mosquitoes or rodents, and odours. Residents of low-income areas reported that solid waste is a 'leading' (85 per cent in Malika) or 'secondary issue' (63 per cent in Pikine) in terms of all the issues facing their area. Malika suffers particularly because it is located just 3 km from Mbeubeuss dump-site. Leachate flows from the dump into the nearby lake, with pollution spreading to local vegetable plots. At the dumpsite there is open burning (including plastic and e-waste), which is especially dangerous for women and children living and working nearby due to high levels of toxic fumes, soil contamination, dermal exposure, and contaminated food and water.

Figure 7.5 Evidence of negative impacts of waste

Waste composition

A comprehensive waste quantification and composition study was carried out in 2014 across the Dakar region (Figure 7.7).[4] This found that 30 per cent of waste by weight consists of 'fine particles': sand and small stones. This heavy material adds to the weight of waste to be collected and transported. Another 24 per cent is organic material. Also making up a large proportion of the waste stream were 'complex' materials (plastic sachets and tetrapac-style layered materials) at 19 per cent, and plastics (both dense and thin) at 9 per cent.

19% of waste is complex materials, such as plastic sachets and tetrapacs

Waste service providers

Waste services are provided by both government and privately run operations. The UCG provides technical and financial support, licenses private providers, and in Dakar, runs some household collection services as well as bulk transport of waste to Mbeubeuss. Together, they help to deal with an estimated 2,500 tonnes of waste generated every day.

There are no accurate estimates of the numbers involved in waste businesses in Dakar. Over 2,000 informal recyclers operate at Mbeubeuss landfill alone. Businesses are male-dominated, often with many young unskilled men working under the supervision of older men involved in the business for several decades. Where women are involved, they often do street cleaning, waste segregation, and recycling (less physical effort and paid at a lower rate), while men are often in charge of waste collection and transport and play a managerial role. Waste collectors and traders had operated for the longest, with all we interviewed having been in the business for at least nine years. Despite the partnership between public services and private collectors, very few businesses we interviewed were formally registered (only one waste collector, none of the waste traders, and no waste pickers).

The system is relatively well organized despite the lack of platforms to facilitate collaboration. There is an active association called Bokk Diom which seven out of 20 service providers we interviewed belonged to (mostly collectors and some waste traders). Bokk Diom is an association of waste pickers and traders formed in 1995 with around 4,000 members each paying an annual membership of CFA 1,000 (Globalrec, n.d.; Fernelius, 2019). It is part of global networks of support through WIEGO. The group lobbied against the attempted closure of Mbeubeuss unless the livelihoods of pickers and traders can be protected and their contribution recognized.

Waste collectors and pickers

Informal service providers play a central role in complementing formal services and recovering waste for recycling (which is not attempted at all by public services). Informal cart operators can cover 80 to 220 households per day. However, making a good income from this business is challenging as subscription is optional for households and people do not always pay reliably. Collectors earn a little more by picking valuable waste out of the mixed waste they collect.

Specialized collectors and waste pickers operate in some neighbourhoods, selling waste on to larger aggregators and recyclers. Respondents were generally ambivalent about their work, with two-thirds overall saying, 'I don't mind them. They are just trying to make a living.' In Cité Lobatt Fall they were viewed even more favourably, with 84 per cent saying, 'they are doing a good job helping us to recycle material'.

At the landfill, waste pickers and recyclers have operated since it opened in 1968. They extract recyclable products, which are sold at the landfill and across the city to waste dealers and recycling companies, including two large Chinese factories (Fernelius, 2019). Male pickers tend to work with more valuable waste, while women (about a quarter of pickers at Mbeubeuss; see WIEGO, 2020) tend to collect food waste used for pigs reared in a nearby neighbourhood (Mattson, 2020).

Together, they recycle approximately 13 per cent of Dakar's waste (WIEGO, 2020), mostly glass, metal, PVC, polystyrene, PET bottles, other plastics, and paper and cardboard. Recycling policies focus primarily on plastics and glass. Metal and e-waste is recycled informally and at a large scale with 78 per cent of e-waste dismantled, 20 per cent segregated and reused, and only 2 per cent eliminated or disposed (Esther, 2012).

Waste trading businesses

The most valuable materials for recyclers were metal, plastics, and paper. Three of the five businesses we interviewed processed materials by compressing, cleaning, or packing them. Ten recycling companies in Dakar focus on plastic, including two companies exporting to China and Vietnam, but for small recycling businesses, 'the lack of financing, the [halt to] plastics export to China, and the lack of demand for recycled plastics mean businesses cannot thrive', according to waste picking and recycling association leader in Malika.

Municipal sweeping services

Street sweeping is only provided in middle- and high-income residential areas. It involves primarily young women and men who are formally employed by the UCG. None of the sweepers interviewed had received any training but they worked with PPE. The waste collected is taken by carts to local informal disposal points. The UCG sweepers pick out valuable waste for sale to supplement their low incomes, but one commented, 'this is forbidden and I risk losing my job'.

Voluntary street clean-ups

In an effort to tackle the remaining waste on the streets, there are occasional clean-up campaigns mentioned by 30 per cent in Pikine and 25 per cent in Malika. These happened 'irregularly', driven by local residents in Pikine. In Malika, 40 per cent said local residents carried this out, and 60 per cent said it was the local government. In Cité Lobatt Fall, 62 per cent mentioned more regular, monthly clean-ups, mostly carried out by the local government with some input from residents.

Working conditions, harassment, and discrimination

Waste workers only benefit from occupational health and safety measures at waste recovery sites run by registered private companies. Protective equipment is often limited to jackets and gloves. Standardized masks and protective glasses are missing, and most operate without health insurance. Our study found that recyclers were more likely to access protective equipment than pickers. At Mbeubeuss, no proper cleaning facilities, clean water, or toilets are available, and burning of e-waste exposes workers to toxic fumes. This also exposes women and children in nearby areas. A waste recycler commented that they face 'high risks due to exposure to hazardous waste and receive no support from the Government ...'.

The majority of pickers, traders, and collectors faced harassment. This is often from the authorities: the police or 'government', but can also be from family members and the community. Street sweepers were the only ones who did not mention any harassment. Women experience additional safety risks especially at the final disposal site, where a third said the risk of assault from other workers was the biggest danger (WIEGO, 2020).

> **Waste workers often face harassment from the authorities**

Box 7.1 Case study: Marème Guèye, female waste recycler

Marème Guèye is a woman in her thirties involved in informal recycling. She reports stigmatization from family and neighbours because of her work, as well as violence and harassment for women at the Mbeubeuss landfill. Provision of medical healthcare remains a critical issue, and informal female recyclers require training to improve their position in the waste recovery chain.

Governance and regulation

Cities and 'communes' across Senegal hold the mandate for solid waste management, receiving varying amounts of technical and financial support through the UCG. At the national level, responsibilities remain scattered between ministries. The budget allocated to waste management in Senegal is CFA 16 bn (€24 m), including CFA 9 bn (€13 m) for the Dakar region alone, but this remains insufficient, and local budgets for waste are embedded into broader environment envelopes. A tax for waste services levied by the city has a low rate of recovery, raising only CFA 3 m (WIEGO, 2020). The UCG supports Dakar Region with around 75 per cent of its operational budget. However, there has not been any rigorous evaluation of operational costs or cost recovery to help make the case for larger budgets. Dakar scores low-medium for financial sustainability in the WasteAware indicators (5F, see Figure 7.9). The financing structure is progressively moving towards taxing private companies in proportion to their waste production.

There is a fairly good level of local institutional coherence on solid waste management in Dakar (medium score on indicator 6L). Although 'user inclusivity' (4U) and 'provider inclusivity' (4P) are high in Dakar, small waste recycling businesses remain excluded from decision-making processes, despite the organized efforts of Bokk Diom.

Mbeubeuss catalyses the public health and ecological crisis around waste in Dakar. The landfill has no legal status, but is managed by the UCG which issues licences for trucks to discharge waste. There have been attempts over time to close the dumpsite, or establish improved recycling operations. This is the intention of the 2019 PROMGEDE programme. A new law also plans to ban single-use or disposable plastic products and implement a 'plastic tax' on non-recyclable materials. These mechanisms could potentially bring additional resources to fund improved waste services and working conditions; however, serious concerns remain among informal businesses that they are not effectively consulted and integrated into the plans, severely limiting their livelihood opportunities.

Conclusion

Collection services in Dakar are valued for their affordability, reliability, and convenience for those who receive them. However, collection is not the only important aspect of a good waste service, and wide inequalities between richer and poorer neighbourhoods are evident when these are taken into account.

The focus of waste management in Dakar has been on collection and disposal. Recovery and recycling businesses are seen as 'peripheral' and entirely separate. Our findings suggest that where collection services are the most effective, there is the least engagement from households in source separation. Conversely, poorer households with the least effective collection services or those relying on disposal points, are more likely to separate waste for recyclers.

The vast majority of waste is collected mixed and is later picked through and sorted by informal businesses, with all the dangers and inefficiencies that entails. If better organized, recycling high-value items could unleash potential for job creation and reducing pollution. Senegal's slow transition to an integrated waste management system means that indiscriminate waste disposal and unsafe recycling still have severe impacts on communities and waste workers. The lack of healthcare, insurance, and legal status puts them at greater risk of disease, harassment, and security issues, especially female recyclers.

The presence of the UCG offers the opportunity for a coordinated response. At the national level, Senegal's green growth roadmap can act as a foundation to generate jobs from recycling. Equally, the presence of an organized and supported association of waste pickers and traders is a strength. WIEGO (2020) call for a number of actions including further capacity building, greater legal recognition for waste work, and better integration with municipal systems. This will require significant changes in perception and approach from all stakeholders, which have been increasingly entrenched in recent years. A new and jointly held vision is sorely needed.

DAKAR

3,835,000 Population of Dakar region   **418,000** Households   **38%** Poor or very poor (2015)   (estimated figures for 2020

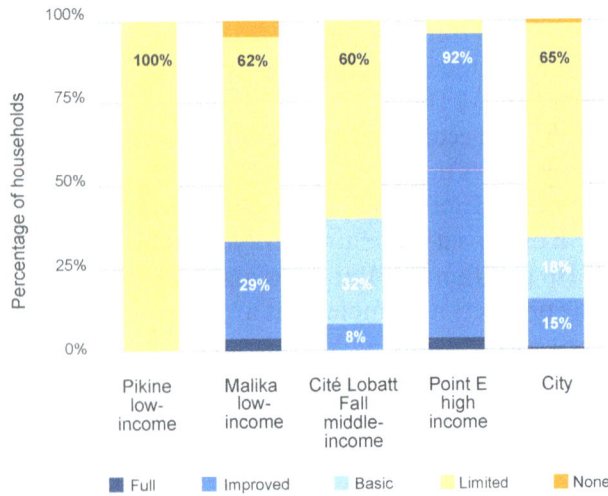

Figure 7.6 Waste services ladder by wealth category

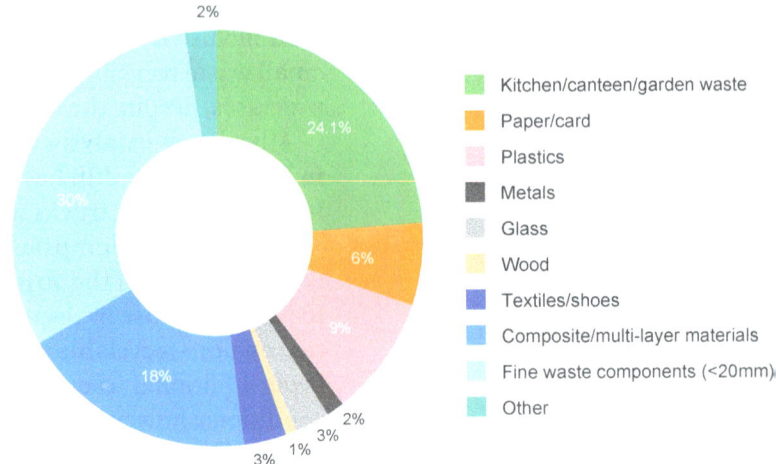

Full   Improved   Basic   Limited   None

Figure 7.7 Composition of household waste, whole city

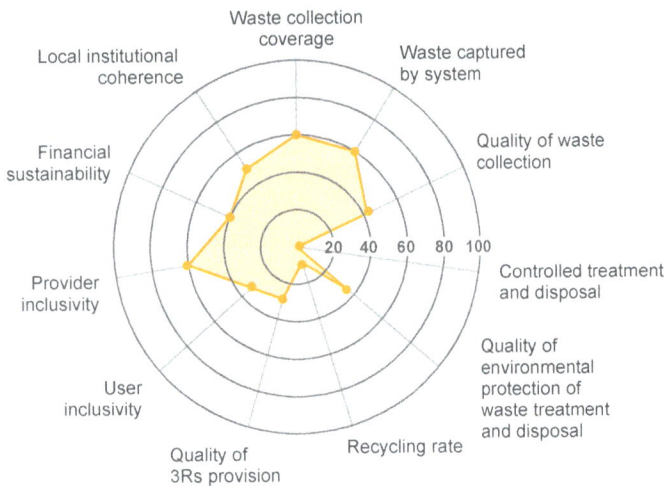

- Kitchen/canteen/garden waste
- Paper/card
- Plastics
- Metals
- Glass
- Wood
- Textiles/shoes
- Composite/multi-layer materials
- Fine waste components (<20mm)
- Other

Figure 7.9 WasteAware indicators

0.58 KG

Average for the whole city.
Waste quantities by socio-economic status were not available from the 2014 study.

Figure 7.8 Average weight of waste per person per day

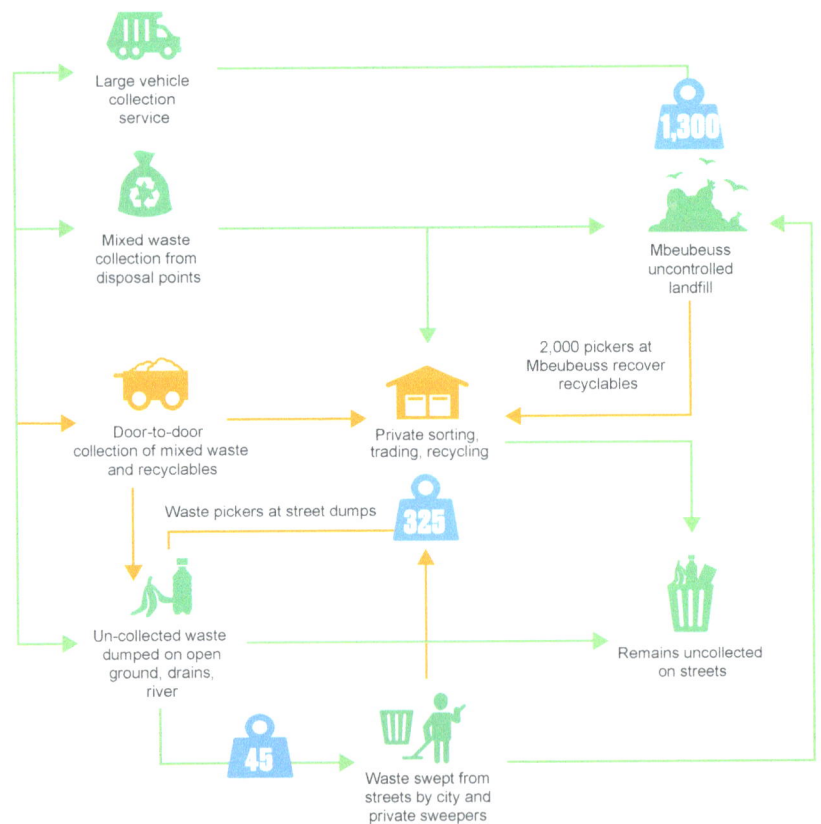

99% of households have access to a waste service (collection or disposal point)

69% of households in low-income neighbourhoods say indiscriminate dumping of waste has a significant impact in their area

13% of the city's waste is recovered and recycled by private/informal waste pickers and traders

Figure 7.10 Municipal waste flows

Key:

- Tonnes per day
- Private service providers
- Municipal/public services

Large vehicle collection service

Mixed waste collection from disposal points

1,300

Mbeubeuss uncontrolled landfill

WASTE GENERATORS

2,500

Door-to-door collection of mixed waste and recyclables

Private sorting, trading, recycling

2,000 pickers at Mbeubeuss recover recyclables

Waste pickers at street dumps

325

Un-collected waste dumped on open ground, drains, river

Remains uncollected on streets

45

Waste swept from streets by city and private sweepers

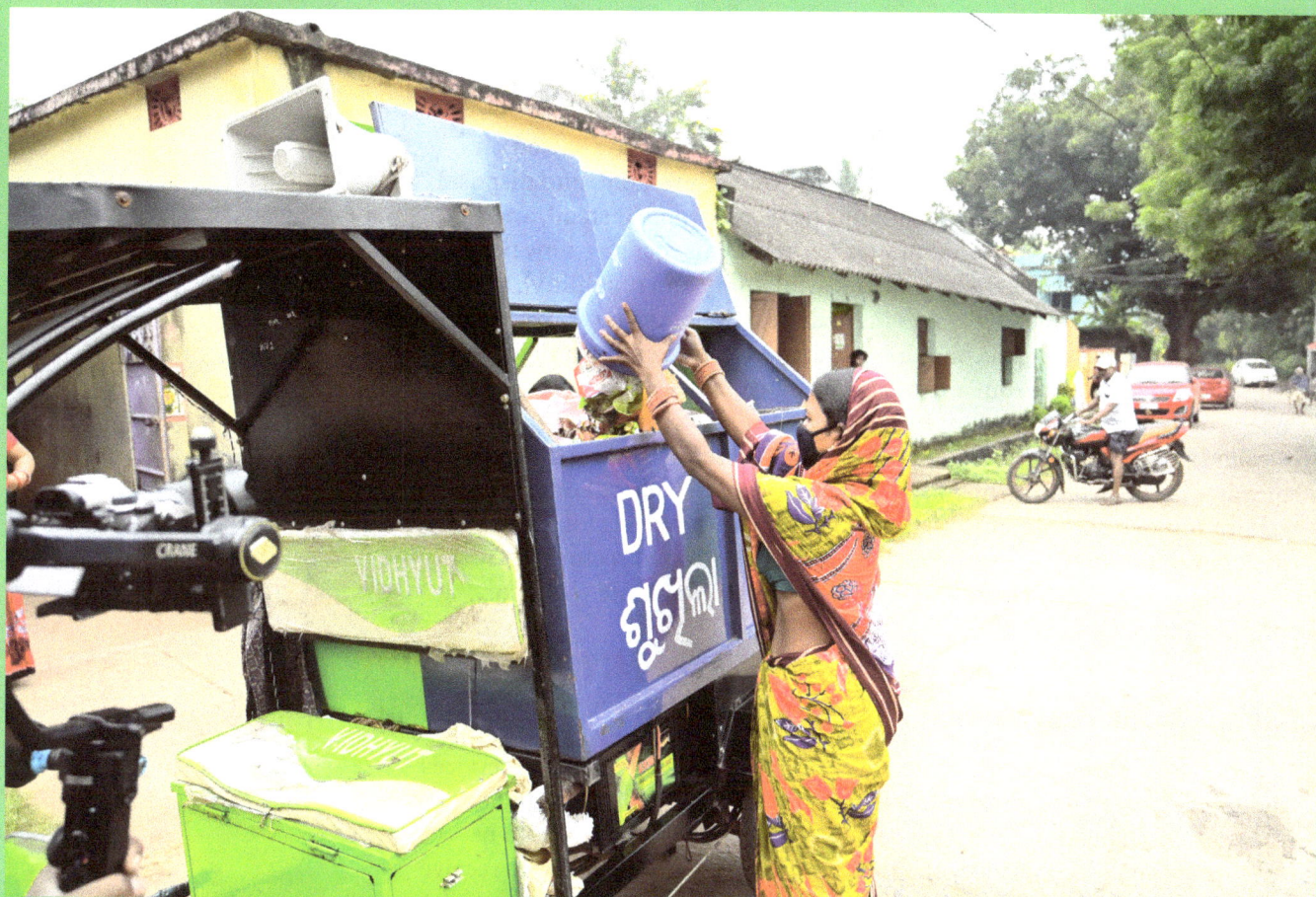

8 PEOPLE-CENTRED WASTE SERVICES

Globally, the waste crisis is huge and causing a significant and damaging impact on the lives of vulnerable people and on the environment. Estimates are that 2 billion people are without waste collection services and 3 billion are without controlled waste disposal (UNEP/ISWA, 2015). Our case studies exposed the realities of these impacts on the lives of the poorest urban residents. They also underlined the lack of reliable official data for monitoring the situation, understanding where progress is being made, and where the biggest gaps remain.

In this chapter, we explore four themes. In each, we consider what it means to take a people-centred approach, and why that is crucial for creating more sustainable solutions for people and the environment. We highlight some examples of what has been tried elsewhere in the world to transform relationships, put people back at the centre of the solution, and move together towards a more sustainable future.

Waste management as a people-centred service

Planning and investments for waste management are often focused on metrics to do with the waste itself: its generation, movement, and disposal, or reuse. The waste services ladder helps focus on people instead, and the attributes of waste services that matter to them. This includes how people interact with and receive the service (its availability and reliability), and how well it deals with waste in people's immediate neighbourhoods. We include separation for recycling because it is fundamental to creating efficiencies for resource recovery. From a service perspective, separation for recycling needs to be convenient and incentivized (financially or in other ways).

Our ladder refines UN-Habitat's proposed ladder by adding the impact of waste in the neighbourhood and broadening definitions about waste separation to better account for the work of the informal sector. Our ladder includes and values, for example, the role of the informal sector in Satkhira where 84 per cent of households routinely separate waste for informal traders.

The waste services ladder focuses on people and the attributes of waste services that matter to them

Gendered access to waste services

Waste services are generally provided to households, and the waste services ladder focuses on *household* provision. We can disaggregate by gender of the household head. We might expect female-headed households to be over-represented in poorer neighbourhoods and thus more likely to receive a poorer service overall. Controlling for this, in Dakar we found that even within low-income neighbourhoods, female-headed households had worse access to waste services than male-headed households (97 per cent had 'limited' access, compared to only 77 per cent of male-headed households).

Within households, impacts are experienced differently between men and women (whether household heads or not). In our case studies in India and Bangladesh, women in slum communities were more likely than men to rate the impacts of waste dumping in their neighbourhood as severe. In focus groups and interviews in all countries, women highlighted the tangible ways in which waste affects their lives, from the stench of rotting food scraps, to flies and pests, and the loss of space for children to play safely. Women tend to have responsibility for the health of their families. In all our case studies they were also responsible for managing waste at the household level, and sometimes (not always) for paying for services. At the same time, women have less voice in decision-making, and actions to address these problems or to promote behaviour change do not fully reflect their concerns.

Women are responsible for managing household waste but have little voice in decision-making

Deep inequalities between rich and poor within cities

Using a waste services ladder allows comparison between neighbourhoods at the city level, and between our four case study cities. Our analysis reveals the deep inequalities in waste service between higher- and lower-income neighbourhoods. These inequalities were especially stark in Kisumu where ability to pay for higher service levels either individually or collectively through estate managers determined the level of service. Similarly, in Dakar, despite the drive for comprehensive waste collection promoted through the national coordinating body UCG, service levels in low-income neighbourhoods remained patchy at best. In the small town of Dhenkanal, there has similarly been a huge drive for comprehensive collection services. Slum dwellers noticed the improvements and enjoyed 'basic' service levels.

As with water and sanitation ladders, we are able to estimate the number of people at citywide level who are without basic services.

This means that their access to a waste service is limited either by poor quality, or because indiscriminate waste dumping still has a significant impact in the neighbourhood. With its comprehensive collection service, Dhenkanal could move easily to higher levels on the ladder with behaviour change campaigns.

Table 8.1 Proportion of people without basic waste services

City	Percentage without basic waste service (%)	Estimated no. of people
Dakar	66	1,638,000
Kisumu	75	379,000
Satkhira	93	158,000
Dhenkanal	61	45,000

People-centred impacts of poor waste management

Our starting point has been waste *services*, but it remains important to monitor waste flows and composition. SDG 11.6.1 requires measuring the 'proportion of municipal solid waste collected and managed in controlled facilities out of total municipal solid waste generated by the city'. The assumption is that if a higher proportion of waste is collected and safely managed, the city as a whole, its people and businesses, will benefit.

Organic waste: plentiful, heavy, and messy. By far the most waste generated by households by weight in every city was kitchen and garden waste: between 57 and 79 per cent. The exception was Dakar, where a lot of waste is 'fine particles' such as sand. While organic matter decomposes fast in the environment, it remains a significant health hazard, encouraging flies and other pests. As soon as kitchen waste mixes with dry recyclables, their value decreases and the cost of recovering those materials in labour, time, and equipment increases significantly. Uncollected and poorly disposed organic waste is also the major source of greenhouse gas emissions from municipal waste. At the same time, it represents a valuable source of nutrients and organic matter that could be captured and returned to the land.

> **As soon as kitchen waste mixes with dry recyclables, their value decreases**

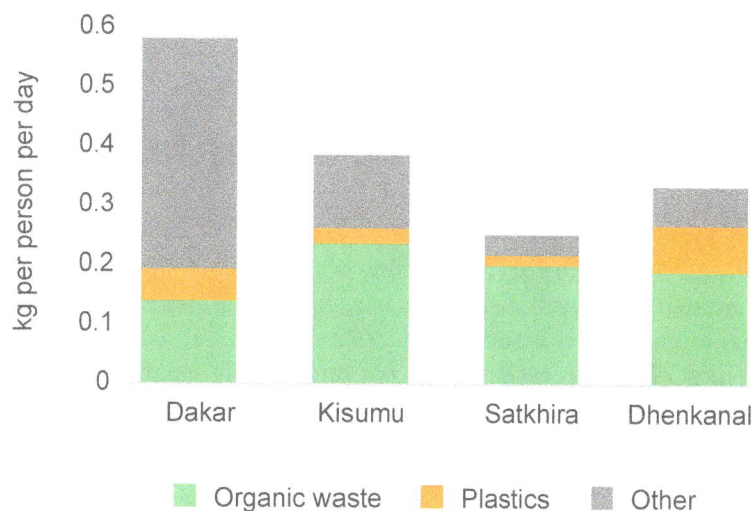

Figure 8.1 Average waste generation and composition per person per day

Plastics: light, bulky, and long-lived. Plastics, both thin film and dense, make up a small proportion of household waste by weight (7-9 per cent, but higher at 23 per cent in Dhenkanal), and yet they currently attract the most attention of all municipal waste streams. This is understandable given that they do not biodegrade, are easily dispersed by wind and water, spreading out across the environment, and contributing to blocked drains, pollution, and waterlogging. There are usually ready markets for dense plastics, and in all cities, this was one of the most valuable materials for recyclers. Thin plastics, however, are not valued. Part of this waste stream, only captured well in the information from Dakar, are product sachets and composite materials. These are widely used for selling small quantities of food, drinks, and household products.

Difficult types of waste and coping strategies: We know that some types of waste were difficult for households to dispose of. In Kisumu, people described the problems they faced in the absence of a waste collection service, in particular for disposing of used menstrual pads and children's nappies. 'Disposable' products have become popular as they have become more affordable in Kenya. Residents said these are hard to burn, which is how they deal with other types of waste. They resorted to throwing them into the pit latrine, which causes problems when that needs to be emptied.

Burning waste is also a coping strategy. It was not mentioned in Bangladesh, but was very common in Kenya. In Dakar we know that while most people's waste is collected, the secondary transfer to the dumpsite fails. Waste is often burned at local dumpsites to try to reduce its volume, smell, and nuisance. However, this burning results in a poorly understood, but 'hazardous cocktail of emissions' released into the atmosphere and onto land (Cook and Velis, 2020).

> **Box 8.1 Sachet economy**
>
> Sachets are a type of flexible plastic packaging made from multiple materials that are 'difficult, if not impossible to recycle'. They are used for small or single portions of food and personal care products such as soap. The market for these packets grew by 19 per cent in just one year in 2017. In 2018, 855 billion sachets were sold globally, with half of this in South-east Asia where they have been marketed to low-income consumers who cannot afford to buy in larger quantities.
>
> *Source:* Greenpeace (2019), Tearfund et al. (2019)

Service providers: closing the gap between collection and recycling

Informal waste workers are at the frontline of recycling. The sector is male-dominated, and in Africa particularly, youth-dominated. These workers are often the only actors in a city to recover materials from waste, supplying larger formal recyclers. They operate entirely separately from municipal services that focus on collection and dumping. Evidence of this contribution has been building over recent years (WIEGO, 2014; Dias and Samson, 2016). For example, in a survey of five global cities, WIEGO found that three-quarters (76 per cent) of waste pickers directly supplied formal businesses with the inputs they need. They point out that waste pickers

Plastics are a small proportion of waste by weight but attract the most attention

Waste pickers
provide inputs
to industries,
create jobs, and
provide a free
environmental
service to local
authorities

provide inputs to industries, they create jobs for themselves and others, and an environmental service at no cost to the local authority.

This was equally the case in the cities we reviewed. In Satkhira, 84 per cent of households give separated waste to traders, as do 22 per cent in Kisumu. In Dakar, waste collectors pick out recyclable waste, and 13 per cent of all waste is recovered for recycling by waste pickers. The local authority played no role at all in these cases. In Dhenkanal, the local authority has set up its own composting and material recovery facilities separately from the existing waste trade. However, waste traders continue to recover far greater volumes of dry recyclables than the municipality.

The motivations for people to work in the waste sector varied. For some, it was one of few options they had to 'make an honest living' in the absence of education, skills, or capital to start another business or find employment. For others, in particular for youth involved, for example in Kenya, it was also a way of making a positive contribution to their community. That meant they were committed to offering a collection service in their neighbourhood, even if they also needed to serve more lucrative better-off households to make it economically viable.

Circular economy opportunities

The opportunities are potentially huge, and beginning to be recognized. A report by the World Economic Forum's Circular Economy Initiative and the African Circular Economy Alliance looked to identify five industries where increased circularity could 'support the economy, jobs and the environment [in Africa] in the long term'. The top two were converting food waste to organic fertilizer, and plastic waste recycling (African Circular Economy Alliance, 2021). However, as Sadan and de Kock (2020) point out in relation to plastic waste, there are a range of economic incentives which drive continuing reliance on plastics, without companies having to bear the consequences.

In Indonesia, the 'waste bank' scheme builds on these kinds of practices by incentivizing households to bring separated waste to recycling centres. A similar, smaller-scale scheme in South Africa has provided a lifeline for workers facing unemployment during the COVID-19 pandemic.

Box 8.2 Waste banks in Indonesia, nationwide success

From 2008 onwards, customers could sell recyclable materials at waste 'banks', with the contribution marked in a bank book. They can either receive the money made from selling the waste, or some other benefit (depending on the bank). The scheme has been supported by the national government since 2012, and by 2018 there were estimated to be 8,036 banks in 34 provinces of Indonesia.

Source: Wijayanti and Suryani (2015), Bahraini (2020)

The people best placed to capitalize on these opportunities are likely to be informal workers who are already skilled in sorting, grading, cleaning, and processing waste to meet the needs of the recycling economy and understand the waste supply chains. New technologies and markets are needed for waste that is currently not valued highly such as thin film plastics, plastic sachets, or large quantities of organic material.

> **Box 8.3 Organized waste buy-back scheme a 'lifeline'**
> **during COVID-19 – South Africa**
>
> South African charity LOCK – Love Our City Klean – has provided a
> lifeline for South Africans, many of whom lost their jobs during the
> country's COVID-19 lockdowns. By bringing recyclable materials to
> LOCK's centres, they receive points on a digital card which they can
> exchange weekly for essential groceries. One participant of the scheme
> said, 'I am not sure if we would be alive without this ... And look how
> clean our streets are'.
>
> *Source:* Harrisberg (2021)

Poor working conditions for informal waste workers

While providing this useful service, informal waste workers face very poor
working conditions. They operate without shade, or access to drinking
water, toilet facilities, or handwashing. This can be an even greater problem
for women while they are menstruating. Workers do not routinely wear
protective equipment, which some reported as hot or constraining, even
when it was available. Waste workers are exposed to hazardous waste and
toxic fumes without protective equipment or health insurance. Workers
deal with dirty, sharp, contaminated, and toxic materials every day.
Airborne illness, animal bites, cuts, bruises, or fungal infections are
common health issues. Time and income are lost to health issues, with
a loss of productivity among workers and, ultimately, shortened life
expectancy (Cook and Velis, 2020).

Some actions are being taken to address these problems collectively. In
Dakar and Satkhira, waste workers were members of associations. These
support workers in a variety of ways including through health insurance.
When rolling this scheme out in four towns in Bangladesh, we found that
it reduced the number of days lost to injury and ill-health by 73 per cent
(Practical Action, 2021). In Dakar, Bokk Diom has been critical in fighting
against the dumpsite's closure to maintain workers' access to their primary
source of livelihood.

Waste workers also routinely face harassment and social discrimination.
This was generally worse for waste pickers. Waste traders face harassment
more from the authorities in terms of their business operations. Collectors
also deal with unhappy customers and community members. Women
face physical and verbal abuse and harassment from the public and other
waste pickers in conflicts over access to waste sources. This can mean
they access less valuable types of waste (as at the dumpsite in Dakar). In
the wider community, people are unwilling to employ waste workers; they
are branded as 'criminals' and can be excluded from community events or
sharing food.

**In Bangladesh,
health insurance
reduced days
of work lost by
73 per cent**

	WASTE GENERATION	COLLECTION & TRANSFER	PRE-PROCESSING	END PROCESSING	END DISPOSAL
UNSAFE PRACTICES	No segregation of waste Exposed hazardous waste Plastic littering	Unsafe handling, logistics and at facilities Manual scavenging Non-compliant trading and poor housekeeping in transportation	Unsafe manual dismantling of e-waste Low-quality segregation of e-components during mechanical processing Manual shredding, melting	Inefficient and dangerous metallurgical processing (e.g. amalgamation, unsound smelting, unsound chemical leaching) Manual shredding, melting	Open burning Open dumping Manual scavenging
HEALTH RISKS	Exposure to contaminated soil and foods (heavy metals, chemicals) Clogged drains causing water-borne diseases Airborne illness, animal bites, cuts, bruises or fungal infections	Cuts, burning Toxic fumes inhalation, causing respiratory diseases Long-lasting development impairment	Exposure to contaminated soil and foods (heavy metals, chemicals) Food and water contamination Cuts, burning Toxic fumes inhalation, causing respiratory diseases Long-lasting development impairment		

Figure 8.2 Prevalent health risks in solid waste management

Source: authors and GIZ (2019)

Governance: structures and capacities for people-centred approaches

Political drivers of waste management

In our case study cities, as with many around the world, local governments focused their limited resources on the issues of greatest political priority. In the first place, this means keeping the streets of their central business district clear of waste. Beyond this, local governments prioritize collection and removal of waste from richer neighbourhoods.

> **Box 8.4 Social protection schemes with informal waste worker cooperatives**
>
> One of the benefits of organizing in cooperatives is that social protection schemes can be organized. ILO (2020) highlights a number of examples including the Cooperative Recuperar in Medellin, Colombia, established in 1983. The cooperative currently has about 1,000 members, 60 per cent of whom are women. The members can access loans, scholarships to continue their studies, and life and accident insurance.

Municipalities often license private collectors but regulation is weak

Realizing that there is a demand for waste collection services, municipalities have licensed the private sector to offer this service. However, this is often done on a free-market basis, and without attempts to ensure services reach all areas of the city. Local authorities also often lack the capacity to supervise and regulate these service providers, meaning provision is variable in its quality and effectiveness.

As populations and the economy of cities grow, and without a strategy for reducing waste, the expansion and poor management of landfill sites

has often become a political issue. In Kisumu, dealing with the Kachok dumpsite became an election pledge for the new County Governor in 2017. In Dakar, the problems are on an even larger scale with several efforts having been made over time to close or reform operations at Mbeubeuss dumpsite.

Limited municipal finances, staffing, and equipment

The financial and organizational capacities of many local governments are severely limited. They may employ a relatively large number of workers, but their ability to operate and maintain fleets of vehicles is constrained, as is their capacity to consider expanding or changing the services they provide. They are rarely successful in gathering fees for waste management from users. Fearing even more indiscriminate dumping, they are often reluctant to charge dumping fees. Even where, as in Kisumu, they have a forward-looking waste strategy with good intentions in terms of reducing waste going to the landfill and increasing recycling, implementation has been difficult.

At one level, local authorities are trying to be people-centred. Their ambition is for a 'clean' city they and their residents can feel proud of, and they are aware that people want a convenient service which removes waste from the neighbourhood and public spaces. In spite of political goodwill, the challenges of operating waste management services translate into public and political anger over poor management of, and polluting, dumpsites.

The exception is Dhenkanal where the municipality took the bold decision, encouraged by the national Clean India Mission, to make significant investments and changes to the waste management system. These were directed not only towards collection but also to recovery and recycling, starting with collection of separated waste.

Failing to build on the expertise and contribution of informal waste workers

Waste pickers and recyclers were not viewed by our case study local authorities as a core part of the solution. Their expertise and knowledge of the waste sector is not valued. The issues they face in trying to expand their services are not addressed. Indeed, the actions of local authorities can easily undermine their access to waste and make their operations more difficult. In Kisumu, the environmental regulator focuses on ensuring businesses pay for expensive licences with conditions designed to protect public health, but which have the effect of dampening the efforts of recyclers. In Dakar, the rates of household separation of waste are close to zero where collection services are the most efficient, which means recyclers are only able to access this waste once it is already mixed at the dumpsite.

In Dhenkanal, waste pickers and traders are beginning to find their access to valuable waste is constrained by the collection and recycling drive of the municipality. As Scheinberg (2012) points out, this strategy is likely to be higher cost and lead to *lower* rates of recycling. She highlights how public authorities or their private contractors 'simply don't know how to valorize materials, don't understand value chains, and lack commercial contacts or experienced traders to help them'.

A far more effective way forwards would be for local governments to support and embrace the work of informal waste workers. In all our case study locations, waste pickers, traders, and collectors were keen for more dialogue with their local authority. This was not happening even where waste actors (or at least some) were organized as with Bokk Diom in Dakar, or KIWAN in Kisumu. A people-focused approach to waste governance and regulation would also provide greater opportunities for community inputs. Communities are already often active in practical ways through clean-up campaigns. But they rarely have an opportunity to input ideas about how waste services could be improved.

The actions of local authorities can undermine the efforts of informal waste workers

Conclusion

A people-centred approach to waste management first calls for a focus on the kinds of waste service households would like. It calls for governance at the municipal level that listens to the suggestions of residents and in particular of women whose voices are rarely heard but who are the key managers of household waste.

Secondly, there is a clear need for local authorities to find ways to integrate with and amplify the effectiveness of the existing vibrant recovery and recycling sectors. These already deal with an important fraction of waste materials. But there are also some materials for which there is no ready market, or which are less easy to collect, transport, and sell. This is the case with both large quantities of organic waste, and with flimsy plastics and complex materials. Other materials are hazardous and need protective systems and processing to treat safely. These are areas of public good which municipalities should focus on.

The environmental impacts of poor waste management are significant. Municipal waste rotting in uncontrolled landfills produces greenhouse gas emissions, as well as releasing toxic gases and polluting the land and water. Plastics leaking into the environment and open burning cause damage to both people and the environment. It is vulnerable urban communities that are on the frontline of much of this pollution. In seeking solutions, they should not be seen as passive recipients, but as a key part of the solution.

9 CONCLUSION

The scale and urgency of the global waste management crisis is beginning to be recognized, with growing initiatives on marine plastics and circular economy. The inclusion of an SDG target on municipal solid waste in 2015 was a welcome step. At the same time, informal waste workers have been organizing themselves, often supported by NGOs. Ongoing research has highlighted the role played by informal workers, which this report builds on. Yet there remains much to do to meet the needs of households without a waste service, and to tackle the rapidly growing volumes of waste openly dumped or burned. The impacts on health, the environment, and the economy are significant.

In this report we put people back at the heart of the waste management picture, with grounded evidence from four contrasting locations. We mapped poor levels of service and highlighted how women and low-income residents bear the greatest burden. We documented the range and scale of informal businesses, and the limited resources and capacities available to municipal and city managers.

Addressing these challenges in a people-centred way requires action by a range of stakeholders. City managers are crucial, having the greatest influence on local actions. Global and national businesses have important responsibilities as both producers of packaging and potential buyers of recyclables. Development institutions and funders can influence the way large-scale initiatives are planned and delivered, and global development assistance needs to increase and be better targeted.

Based on these insights, our recommendations focus on four areas:

Waste management as a people-centred service

- Targets should be set at local and national levels to improve the proportion of people with access to *at least basic* waste management services. Similarly, waste management should be included as a 'basic service' under SDG 1.4.
- Access to waste services should be measured using a ladder similar to the approach taken for water, sanitation, and hygiene (SDG 6). Results must be disaggregated to highlight differences by wealth and gender.

Tackling the waste that affects people the most

- Priority should be given to encouraging and supporting households to safely manage organic kitchen waste, starting with keeping this waste separate. This has many benefits throughout the waste value chain, and helps households deal with material that can quickly cause problems.
- Solutions should be found for recovering waste streams that currently have no or limited market value for recycling, including particular types of plastics. Similarly, solutions are needed for safe disposal of potentially hazardous or private materials, such as used nappies or sanitary pads, and electronic items.

Improving the lives and working conditions of informal waste workers

- The contribution and expertise of informal and semi-formal waste collection, recycling, and trading businesses must be recognized and valued. These businesses can be supported to provide a better, safer service with improved livelihoods, dignity, and working conditions.
- The additional layers of discrimination and abuse faced by women in waste businesses should be tackled to find routes to empowerment through awareness raising, practical support, and bringing women together in cooperatives and other associations to help build their capacity collectively.
- Partnerships are needed so that municipalities and cities provide opportunities for informal businesses to grow and avoid undermining access to sources of waste or markets for recyclables.

Greater voice in decision-making for those most affected

- At both national and global levels, waste policies need to focus not only on environmental benefits, but also on improving the lives of the poorest communities.
- Local authorities and recycling companies should establish forums, bringing in expertise from informal waste businesses and the passion and dynamism of youth, integrating them effectively into waste management systems. Informal sector businesses need support to build effective associations and cooperatives which can represent their interests, build trust with city authorities, and meet the needs of their members.

NOTES

Chapter 2

1. Words are important in this case. At the First World Conference of Waste Pickers, held in Colombia in 2008, a consensus was reached to use the generic term 'waste picker' in English (but, in specific contexts, to use the term preferred by the local waste-picking community) and avoid the term 'scavenger' due to its derogatory meaning.

Chapter 4

1. A study in 2018 found around 480 informal waste and sanitation workers in Faridpur, which is a slightly larger town than Satkhira.
2. Assuming that households who say they separate this waste for recycling still throw away about 20 per cent of that type of waste, with 80 per cent going to recycling.
3. As confirmed in the Satkhira Municipality website: <https://www.satkhiramunicipality.org.bd/services.php?home_id=18>.
4. The national minimum wage is BDT 1500 per month, which equates to just US$17.70.

Chapter 5

1. Waste traders estimate there are 10 medium-sized businesses (who could employ 10 people on average) and 20 smaller businesses (five people on average). In addition, we can assume there are at least 100 waste pickers.

Chapter 6

1. The 2019 census reports 20 towns of this size, but this reports just the 'core' population rather than 'core' and 'peri-urban' which were included in 1999 and 2009, so the figures are not directly comparable.
2. The Kisumu County Integrated Development Plan 2018–2022 clarifies that 'The City of Kisumu covers ... 14 of the 35 wards of the County' (page 109) which are (page 9) all wards in Kisumu Central and Kisumu East sub-counties, plus the following wards in Kisumu West: South West Kisumu, Central Kisumu and North Kisumu.

Our figure for the city's population is based on these wards from the 2019 census.

3. Based on a classification of the city's sub-locations into high, middle, middle–low, and low income, using population figures from the 2019 census.

4. This agrees with findings from a study using a representative sample from early 2018, which found that 62 per cent of households were not subscribed to any waste collection service.

5. Also see video by ICLEI about this river from 2019 <https://www.youtube.com/watch?v=N1PP4EjUAnM&t=114s> [accessed 1 August 2021].

6. UN-Habitat's WasteWise Cities tool does not specify where to categorize sanitary towels, but includes children's nappies in the 'other' category.

7. Our estimate for household waste generation is around 194 tonnes per day which is similar to the 210 tonnes a day by KISWAMP. They assumed a generation rate of 0.5 kg per person per day, while our study revealed lower quantities especially in low-income neighbour-hoods. KISWAMP estimates that a further 175 tonnes per day comes from businesses. UN-Habitat's studies suggest businesses generate only an additional 30 per cent on top of household waste. They use this proportion in Nairobi. Applied here gives a total waste per day of 252 tonnes.

Chapter 7

1. Based on compilation from studies carried out by UCG in 2014 in Dakar Region. See e.g. UCG (2014).

2. For estimates at citywide level we weighted cases according to the wealth categories for urban Dakar Region as published in ANSD (2015).

3. In 2006, Rouyat (2006) estimates collection rates to range between 15 and 20 per cent in Njamena, 23 per cent in Ouagadougou, 20–30 per cent in Nouakchott and 35 per cent in Dakar.

4. See UCG (2014) for an example from Dakar and UCG (2016) for the national picture.

REFERENCES

Abul, S. (2010) 'Environmental and health impact of solid waste disposal at Mangwaneni dumpsite in Manzini: Swaziland', *Journal of Sustainable Development in Africa* 12(7) <https://jsd-africa.com/Jsda/V12N07_Winter2010_A/article12_7.htm>.

African Circular Economy Alliance (2021) *Five Big Bets for the Circular Economy in Africa* [pdf], World Economic Forum, Geneva <https://www.weforum.org/reports/five-big-bets-for-the-circular-economy-in-africa-african-circular-economy-alliance> [accessed 27 July 2021].

Ali, A., Iqbal N.T. and Sadiq K. (2016) 'Environmental enteropathy', *Current Opinion in Gastroenterology* 32(1): 12–17 <https://doi.org/10.1097/MOG.0000000000000226>.

Ali, S.M. (2018) 'Recognising gender issues in the management of urban waste', *Solid waste management: a collection of synthesis notes* [online], Note no. 5, <https://hdl.handle.net/2134/30255> [accessed 27 July 2021].

ANSD (2015) *Pauvreté et Condition de Vie des Menages* [pdf], Agence Nationale de la Statistique et de la Demographie, Senegal <http://www.ansd.sn/ressources/publications/PAUVRETE%20ET%20CONDITION%20DE%20VIE%20DES%20MENAGES-DEF-VRC-VF.pdf> [accessed 27 July 2021].

ANSD (2016) *Mapping the Poor in Senegal: Technical Report* [pdf], Agence Nationale de la Statistique et de la Demographie, Senegal <https://www.ansd.sn/ressources/publications/SEN_PovMap_160512_rapport%20Version%20Anglaise.pdf> [accessed 27 July 2021].

Awuor, F.O., Nyakinya, B., Oloo, J., Oloko, M. and Agong, S.G. (2019) 'How did Kachok dumpsite in Kisumu City develop into a crisis?' *Urban Forum* 30: 115–31 <https://doi.org/10.1007/s12132-018-9342-7>.

Bahadur, A. and Dodman, D. (2021) *Urban Climate Resilience: A Landscape Review: India, Bangladesh and Kenya*, IIED, London.

Bahraini, A. (2020) 'Waste bank program to support Indonesia Clean-from-Waste 2025' [blog], *Waste4Change*, <https://waste4change.com/blog/waste-bank-to-support-indonesia-clean-from-waste-2025/> [accessed 27 July 2021].

Banna, F. (2017) *Municipal Solid Waste Management in Burkina Faso: Diagnostic and Recommendations*, World Bank, Washington, DC.

Bhutta, Z.A., Guerrant, R.L. and Nelson, C.A. (2017) 'Neurodevelopment, nutrition, and Inflammation: the evolving global child health landscape', *Pediatrics* 139 (Supplement 1): S12–S22 <https://doi.org/10.1542/peds.2016-2828D>.

Casey, J. (2016) *Technology and the Future of Work: Experiences of Informal Waste Workers and Street Vendors in Dhaka, Lima, and Nairobi* [pdf], Practical Action <https://www.wiego.org/sites/default/files/resources/files/Tech_Justice_Practical_Action.pdf> [accessed 27 July 2021].

Chvatal, J. (2010) 'A study of waste management policy implications for landfill waste salvagers in the Western Cape', MA thesis, University of Cape Town, South Africa.

CIWM and WasteAid (2018) 'From the land to the sea' [pdf], <https://wasteaid.org/wp-content/uploads/2018/03/From-the-Land-to-the-Sea.pdf> [accessed 27 July 2021].

Cook, E. and Velis, C.A. (2020) *Global Review on Safer End of Engineered Life*, Royal Academy of Engineering, London <https://doi.org/10.5518/100/58>.

CWG and GIZ (2011) *The Economics of the Informal Sector in Solid Waste Management*, Collaborative Working Group on Solid Management in Low- and Middle-Income Countries.

Czerkinsky, C. and Holmgren, J. (2015) 'Vaccines against enteric infections for the developing world', *Philosophic Transactions of the Royal Society B* 370(1671) <https://doi.org/10.1098/rstb.2015.0142>.

Dias, S. and Fernandez, L. (2013) 'Wastepickers: a gendered perspective', in *Powerful Synergies: Gender Equality, Economic Development and Environmental Sustainability*, United Nations Development Programme, New York, pp. 153–55.

Dias, S.M. and Samson, M. (2016) *Informal Economy Monitoring Study Sector Report: Waste Pickers* [pdf], Women in Informal Employment, Globalizing and Organizing, Cambridge, MA, <https://www.wiego.org/sites/default/files/publications/files/Dias-Samson-IEMS-Waste-Picker-Sector-Report.pdf> [accessed 27 July 2021].

Duggan, B., Prior, R. and Sterling, J. (2017) 'Death toll rises in Ethiopian trash dump landslide', *CNN*, 15 March, <http://edition.cnn.com/2017/03/15/africa/ethiopia-trash-landslide-death-toll/index.html> [accessed 27 July 2021].

Ehui, S (2020) '"You only see trash. We see a treasure trove", why waste management in Senegal is a critical step toward sustainability' [blog], *World Bank Blogs*, <https://blogs.worldbank.org/nasikiliza/you-only-see-trash-we-see-treasure-trove-why-waste-management-senegal-critical-step> [accessed 27 July 2021].

Ellen MacArthur Foundation (2019) *Completing the Picture: How the Circular Economy Tackles Climate Change V.3* [pdf], <https://www.ellenmacarthurfoundation.org/assets/downloads/Completing_The_Picture_How_The_Circular_Economy-_Tackles_Climate_Change_V3_26_September.pdf> [accessed 27 July 2021].

Environmental Justice Atlas (2019a) 'Multinational takeover threatens the livelihood of the Zabbaleen, Egypt' [online], *EJAtlas*, <https://ejatlas.org/conflict/cairos-zabbaleen-continue-facing-hardships-after-the-multinational-waste-management-contracts-have-to-an-end-in-2017> [accessed 27 July 2021].

Environmental Justice Atlas (2019b) 'The new reppie incinerator at Koshe Landfill in Addis Ababa, Ethiopia leaves the wastepickers without livelihood' [online], *EJAtlas*, <https://ejatlas.org/conflict/the-new-reppie-incinerator-at-koshe-landfill-in-addis-ababa-ethiopia-leaves-the-wastepickers-without-livelihood>[accessed 27 July 2021].

Fargier, M (2015) Imperial College UG4 thesis/ research paper

Fergutz, O., Dias, S. and Mitlin, D. (2011) 'Developing urban waste management in Brazil with waste picker organizations', *Environment and Urbanization* 23(2): 597–608 <https://doi.org/10.1177/0956247811418742>.

Fernelius, K.J. (2019) 'The global garbage economy begins (and ends) in this Senegalese dump, *The Nation*, 31 December, <https://www.thenation.com/article/archive/garbage-china-senegal-economy/> [accessed 27 July 2021].

Gakungu, N.K., Gitau, A.N., Njoroge, B.N.K. and Kimani, M.W. (2012) 'Solid waste management in Kenya: a case study of public technical training institutions', *ICASTOR Journal of Engineering* 5(3): 127–38.

Ghosh, S.K. (2016) 'Swachhaa Bharat Mission (SBM) – a paradigm shift in waste management and cleanliness in India', *Procedia Environmental Sciences* 35: 15–27 <https://doi.org/10.1016/j.proenv.2016.07.002>.

Gilmartin, A.A. and Petri, W.A. (2015) 'Exploring the role of environmental enteropathy in malnutrition, infant development and oral vaccine response', *Philosophic Transactions of the Royal Society B* 370(1671) <https://dx.doi.org/10.1098%2Frstb.2014.0143>.

Globalrec (n.d.) *Association Bokk Diom des Récupérateurs et recycleurs de Mbeubeuss* [website], Global Alliance of Waste Pickers <https://globalrec.org/organization/association-bok-diom-des-recuperateurs-et-recycleurs-de-mbeubeuss/> [accessed 28 July 2021].

GoB (2019) *Country Report, Bangladesh* [pdf], Government of Bangladesh, for Ninth Regional 3R Forum in Asia and the Pacific, <https://www.uncrd.or.jp/content/documents/7530Combined-Front%20page+report-Bangladesh.pdf> [accessed 28 July 2021].

Godfrey, L. (2018) *Africa Waste Management Outlook* [pdf], United Nations Environment Programme <https://wedocs.unep.org/handle/20.500.11822/25514> [accessed 28 July 2021].

Gower, R. and Schroeder, P. (2018) *Cost-Benefit Assessment of Community-Based Recycling and Waste Management in Pakistan*, Tearfund and Institute of Development Studies, London and Brighton.

Greenpeace (2019) 'Throwing away the future: how companies still have it wrong on plastic pollution "solutions"' [online], <https://www.breakfreefromplastic.org/bffp_reports/throwing-away-the-future-how-companies-still-have-it-wrong-on-plastic-pollution-solutions/> [accessed 28 July 2021].

Gumbihi, H. (2013) 'Unmasking the trashlords of Dandora', *The Standard*, 26 October, <http://www.standardmedia.co.ke/entertainment/the-standard/2000114387/unmasking-the-trashlords-of-dandora> [accessed 28 July 2021].

Gunsilius, E., Spies, S., García-Cortés, S., Medina, M., Dias, S. and Scheinberg, A. (2011) *Recovering Resources, Creating Opportunities: Integrating the Informal Sector into Solid Waste Management*, Deutsche Gesellschaft für Internationale Zusammenarbeit (GIZ), Eschborn.

Haan, H.C., Coad, A. and Lardinois, I. (1998) *Municipal Waste Management: Involving Micro-and-Small Enterprises. Guidelines for Municipal Managers*, International Training Centre of the ILO, SKAT, WASTE, Turin, Italy.

Harrisberg, K. (2021) 'The South African "trash for cash" scheme that became a lockdown lifeline' [blog], *World Economic Forum*, <https://www.weforum.org/agenda/2021/04/trash-for-cash-south-africans-currency-environment-covid-lockdown/> [accessed 28 July 2021].

Herbert, L. (2007) *Centenary History of Waste and Waste Managers in London and South East* [pdf], The Chartered Institution of Wastes Management, Northampton.

Hoornweg, D. and Bhada-Tata, P. (2012) *What a Waste: A Global Review of Solid Waste Management*, Urban development series; knowledge papers no. 15, World Bank, Washington, DC <https://openknowledge.worldbank.org/handle/10986/17388> [accessed 28 July 2021].

Hunt, C. (1996) 'Child waste pickers in India: the occupation and its health risks', *Environment and Urbanization* 8(2): 111–18 <https://doi.org/10.1177/095624789600800209>.

ILO (2020) 'Waste pickers' cooperatives and social and solidarity economy organizations' [pdf], Cooperatives and the World of Work no. 12, International Labour Office, Geneva <https://www.ilo.org/wcmsp5/groups/public/---ed_emp/---emp_ent/---coop/documents/publication/wcms_715845.pdf> [accessed 28 July 2021].

ISWA (2016) *A Roadmap for Closing Waste Dumpsites, The World's Most Polluted Places* [pdf], International Solid Waste Association, Vienna, <http://www.wastelessfuture.com/pdf/ISWA%20ROADMAP%20V070916.pdf> [accessed 28 July 2021].

Ivanova, D., Stadler K., Steen-Olsen K., Wood R., Vita G., Tukker A. and Hertwich E.G. (2015) 'Environmental impact assessment of household consumption', *Journal of Industrial Ecology* 20: 526–36 <https://doi.org/10.1111/jiec.12371>.

Jambeck, J.R., Geyerm, R., Wilcox, C., Siegler, T.R., Perryman, M., Andrady, A., Narayan, R. and Law, K.L. (2015) 'Plastic waste inputs from land into the ocean', *Science* 347(6223): 768–71 <https://doi.org/10.1126/science.1260352>.

Jerie, S. (2016) 'Occupational risks associated with solid waste management in the informal sector of Gweru, Zimbabwe', *Journal of Environmental and Public Health* <https://doi.org/10.1155/2016/9024160>.

John, C.C., Black, M.M, and Nelson, C.A (2017) 'Neurodevelopment: The Impact of Nutrition and Inflammation During Early to Middle Childhood in Low Resource Settings', *Pediatrics* vol. 139,Suppl 1 (2017): S59-S71. doi:10.1542/peds.2016-2828H.

Kaza, S., Yao, L.C., Bhada-Tata, P. and Van Woerden, F. (2018) *What a Waste 2.0: A Global Snapshot of Solid Waste Management to 2050*, World Bank, Washington, DC, <https://openknowledge.worldbank.org/handle/10986/30317> [accessed 28 July 2021].

Kimani, N.G. (2005) 'Blood lead levels in Kenya: a case study for children and adolescents in selected areas of Nairobi and Olkalou, Nyandarua District, Nairobi, Kenya' [pdf], Kenyatta University, Nairobi, <https://docplayer.net/13037127-Blood-lead-levels-in-kenya-a-case-study-for-children-and-adolescents-in-selected-areas-of-nairobi-and-olkalou-nyandarua-district.html> [accessed 12 August 2021].

Kistler, A. and Muffett, C. (eds) (2019) *Plastic & Climate: The Hidden Costs of a Plastic Planet* [pdf], Center for International Environmental Law, <https://www.ciel.org/wp-content/uploads/2019/05/Plastic-and-Climate-FINAL-2019.pdf> [accessed 28 July 2021].

Kisumu County (2017) *Kisumu Integrated Solid Waste Management Plan (KISWaMP) by horizon 2030* [pdf], County Government of Kisumu <https://www.kisumu.go.ke/wp-content/uploads/2019/08/Updated-KISWAMP-Feb-2018-.pdf> [accessed 28 July 2021].

Kisumu County (2018) *Kisumu County Integrated Development Plan II 2018-2022* [pdf], County Government of Kisumu <https://www.kisumu.go.ke/wp-content/uploads/2018/11/Kisumu-County-CIDP-II-2018-2022.pdf> [accessed 28 July 2021].

KNBS (2017) 'Poverty estimates' [online], *Kenya National Bureau of Statistics*, Nairobi, <https://kenya.opendataforafrica.org/urwhbig/poverty-estimates?region=1000270-kisumu> [accessed 28 July 2021].

KNBS (2019) 'Kenya population and housing census, volume II, distribution of population by administrative units' [online], Kenya National Bureau of Statistics, Nairobi <https://www.knbs.or.ke/?wpdmpro=2019-kenya-population-and-housing-census-volume-ii-distribution-of-population-by-administrative-units> [accessed 28 July 2021].

Kodros, J.K, Wiedinmyer, C., Ford, B., Cucinotta, R., Gan, R., Magzamen, S. and Pierce, J.R. (2016) 'Global burden of mortalities due to chronic exposure to ambient PM2.5 from open combustion of domestic waste', *Environmental Research Letters* 11(124022) <http://dx.doi.org/10.1088/1748-9326/11/12/124022>.

Korpe, P.S. and Petri, W.A. Jr (2012) 'Environmental enteropathy: critical implications of a poorly understood condition', *Trends in Molecular Medicine* 18(6): 328–36 <http://dx.doi.org/10.1016/j.molmed.2012.04.007>.

Kotelawala, H., (2017) 'Sri Lanka death toll rises in garbage dump collapse' [online], *New York Times*, 17 April, <https://www.nytimes.com/2017/04/17/world/asia/sri-lanka-garbage-dump.html> [accessed 28 July 2021].

Kretzmann, S. (2020) 'Tragic landfill conflict fouls Cape Town's air' [online], *Ground Up*, 27 February, <https://www.groundup.org.za/article/tragic-landfill-conflict-fouls-city-air> [accessed 28 July 2021].

Lakshmi, R. (2016) 'A burning mountain of trash in Mumbai fuels middle-class outcry' [online], *Washington Post*, 15 April, <https://www.washingtonpost.com/world/asia_pacific/a-burning-mountain-of-trash-in-mumbai-fuels-middle-class-outcry/2016/04/11/28336511-33b4-437d-8f4d-f53dba9fdf0e_story.html> [accessed 28 July 2021].

Lerpiniere, D., Wilson, D.C., Velis, C., Evans, B., Voss, H. and Moodley, K. (2014) *A Review of International Development Co-operation in Solid Waste Management 2014*, ISWA, Vienna.

Madsen, C. (2006) 'Feminizing waste: waste-picking as an empowerment opportunity for women and children in Impoverished communities', *Colorado Journal of Environmental Law and Policy*, 17: 165.

Marello, M. and Helwege, A. (2017) 'Solid waste management and social inclusion of waste pickers: opportunities and challenges', *Latin American Perspectives* <https://doi.org/10.1177/0094582X17726083>.

Mattson, R.A. (2020) 'Labor rights, gender, and value at Senegal's Mbeubeuss dump' [online], *ArcGIS StoryMaps*, <https://storymaps.arcgis.com/stories/1af419fe7a8542258fe06e8dd4c5bf09> [accessed 28 July 2021].

Mberu, B., Muindi, K., and Faye, C. (2018) 'Improving solid waste management practices and addressing associated health risks in Dakar, Senegal' [online], *Urban ARK Briefing* 13, IIED, <https://pubs.iied.org/g04299> [accessed 28 July 2021].

Medina, M. (2007) *The World's Scavengers*, AltaMira Press, Lanham.

MEFP/ANSD (2015) *Projection de la population du Sénégal 2013-2063* [pdf], Ministere de L'Economie, des Finances et du Plan, et Agence Nationale de la Statistique et de la Démographie, Dakar, <http://www.ansd.sn/ressources/publications/Rapport%20final%20Projection%20-BECPD__12%20Aout_2015__DSDS_vfN.pdf> [accessed 28 July 2021].

MoEF (2015) *Intended Nationally Determined Contributions* [pdf], Ministry of Environment and Forests, Bangladesh <https://www4.unfccc.int/sites/ndcstaging/PublishedDocuments/Bangladesh%20First/INDC_2015_of_Bangladesh.pdf> [accessed 28 July 2021].

MoEF (2021) *National Sustainable Waste Management Policy, Revised Draft* [pdf], Ministry of Environment and Forestry, Kenya, <http://www.environment.go.ke/wp-content/uploads/2021/03/FINAL-National-Waste-Policy-March-2020.pdf> [accessed 28 July 2021].

MoENR (2015) *Kenya's Intended Nationally Determined Contribution* [pdf], Ministry of Environment and Natural Resources, Kenya, <https://www4.unfccc.int/sites/ndcstaging/PublishedDocuments/Kenya%20First/Kenya_NDC_20150723.pdf> [accessed 28 July 2021].

MoENR (2017) 'Nationally appropriate mitigation action on a circular economy solid waste management approach for urban areas in Kenya' [online], Ministry of Environment and Natural Resources, Kenya, and UNDP, New York <https://www.undp.org/publications/nama-circular-economy-solid-waste-management-approach-urban-areas-kenya> [accessed 28 July 2021].

Muindi, K., Mberu, B., Aboderin, I., Haregu, T. and Amugsi, D. (2016) *Conflict and Crime in Municipal Solid Waste Management: Evidence from Mombasa and Nairobi*, Kenya Working Paper no. 13, African Population and Health Research Centre (APHRC).

Müller, E., Boni, H. and Wittman, A. (2012) *Les Déchets Solides Municipaux en Afrique de l'Ouest : Entre Pratiques Informelles, Privatisation Et Amélioration Du Service Public* [pdf], Seventh Framework Progamme, <https://www.pseau.org/outils/ouvrages/empa_enda_les_dechets_solides_municipaux_en_afrique_de_l_ouest_entre_pratiques_informelles_privatisation_et_amelioration_du_service_public_2012.pdf> [accessed 4 August 2021].

Mushonga, B., Habarugira, G., Musabyemungu, A., Udahemuka, J.C., Jaja, F.I. and Pepe, D. (2015) 'Investigations of foreign bodies in the fore-stomach of cattle at Ngoma slaughterhouse, Rwanda', *Journal of South African Veterinary Association* 86(1) <https://doi.org/10.4102/jsava.v86i1.1233>.

Osei, F.B. and Duker, A.A. (2008) 'Spatial and demographic patterns of cholera in Ashanti region – Ghana', *International Journal of Health Geographics* 44(7) <https://doi.org/10.1186/1476-072X-7-44>.

Parsons, S., Maassen, A. and Glavin, M. (2019) 'Urban transformations: in Pune, India, waste pickers go from trash to treasure' [online], World Resources Institute, 25 March, <https://www.wri.org/insights/urban-transformations-pune-india-waste-pickers-go-trash-treasure> [accessed 28 July 2021].

Practical Action (2015) *Baseline Study on Sanitation Service Delivery in Angul and Dhenkanal Municipalities of Odisha*, Practical Action, Bhubaneswar.

Practical Action (2016) *City-wide Situation Analysis of Solid Waste and Faecal Sludge Management in Satkhira Municipality*, Practical Action, Dhaka.

Practical Action (2021) *Dignifying Lives: Final Project Report*, Practical Action, Dhaka.

Prendergast, A. and Kelly, P. (2012) 'Enteropathies in the developing world: neglected effects on global health', *The American Journal of Tropical Medicine and Hygiene* 86(5): 756–63 <https://doi.org/10.4269/ajtmh.2012.11-0743>.

Reyna-Bensusan, N., Wilson, D.C., Davy, P.M., Fuller, G.W., Fowler, G.D. and Smith. S.R. (2019) 'Experimental measurements of black carbon emission factors to estimate the global impact of uncontrolled burning of waste', *Atmospheric Environment*, 213: 629–39 <https://doi.org/10.1016/j.atmosenv.2019.06.047>.

Rouyat, J., Broutin, C., Rachmuhl, V., Gueye, A., Torrasani, V. and Ka, I. (2006) *La Gestion des Ordures Ménagères dans les Villes Secondaires du Sénégal* [pdf], Gret <https://www.gret.org/wp-content/uploads/07766.pdf> [accessed 4 August 2021].

Sadan, Z. and De Kock, L. (2020) *Plastics: Facts and Futures: Moving Beyond Pollution Management Towards a Circular Plastics Economy in South Africa* [pdf], WWF South Africa, Cape Town, <https://wwfafrica.awsassets.panda.org/downloads/wwf_plastics_report_final_2nov2020.pdf> [accessed 28 July 2021].

Scheinberg, A., Wilson, D.C. and Rodic, L. (2010) *Solid Waste Management in the World's Cities*, Earthscan for UN-Habitat, London and Washington, DC.

Scheinberg, A. (2012) *Informal Sector Integration and High Performance Recycling: Evidence from 20 Cities* [pdf], WIEGO Working Paper (Urban Policies) no. 23, <https://www.wiego.org/sites/default/files/publications/files/Scheinberg_WIEGO_WP23.pdf> [accessed 28 July 2021].

Seadon, J., Modak, P. and Periathamby, A. (2017) *Asia Waste Management Outlook*, UNEP, Nairobi.

Singh, R. (2021) *Integration of Informal Sector in Solid Waste Management: Strategies and Approaches* [pdf], Centre for Science and Environment, New Delhi <https://www.cseindia.org/content/downloadreports/10886> [accessed 28 July 2021].

Singh, S. (2020) 'Solid waste management in urban India: imperatives for improvement', Occasional Paper no. 283, Observer Research Foundation, <https://www.orfonline.org/research/solid-waste-management-in-urban-india-imperatives-for-improvement-77129/> [accessed 28 July 2021].

SOENECS Ltd (2016) Report for the London Waste and Recycling Board (LWARB) and the Greater London Authority, <https://www.lwarb.gov.uk/wp-content/uploads/2016/09/LWARB-International-recycling-rate-comparison.pdf> [accessed 22/10/2019].

Stevens, L., Mehrab, U.G. and Kumar Saha, U. (2019) 'Creating the working conditions for health, dignity and opportunity', Policy Brief, Practical Action, Rugby <https://infohub.practicalaction.org/bitstream/handle/11283/622054/Health-Dignity-Opportunity_policy-brief_Dec19.pdf?sequence=4&isAllowed=y> [accessed 28 July 2021].

Stocker, T. (ed.) *Climate Change 2013: The Physical Science Basis* [pdf], Working Group I Contribution to the Fifth Assessment Report of the Intergovernmental Panel on Climate Change, New York.

Tearfund, Fauna & Flora International, WasteAid and Institute of Development Studies (2019) *No Time to Waste: Tackling the Plastic Pollution Crisis Before it's too Late* [pdf], Tearfund, London <https://learn.tearfund.org/-/media/learn/resources/reports/2019-tearfund-consortium-no-time-to-waste-en.pdf> [accessed 28 July 2021].

Tiruneh, R. and Yesuwork, H. (2010) 'Occurrence of rumen foreign bodies in sheep and goats slaughtered at the Addis Ababa Municipality Abattoir', *Ethiopian Veterinary Journal*, 14(1): 91–100 <https://www.ajol.info/index.php/evj/article/view/63872>.

UCG (2014) *Rapport de la Campagne Nationale de Caractérisation des Déchets Solides*, Saison Humide, Région de Dakar, Zone no. 1 (Dakar Plateau, Gueule Tapée / Fass / Colobane, Médina) Ministère de la Gouvernance locale, du Développement, et de l'Aménagement du Territoire et Unité de Coordination de la Gestion des déchets solides (UCG), Dakar.

UCG (2016) *Rapport de la campagne nationale de caractérisation des ordures ménagères et assimilées (2014/2015/2016) Rapport National* [online], Ministère de la Gouvernance locale, du Développement, et de l'Aménagement du Territoire et UCG, Dakar, <https://www.waste-ndc.pro/wp-content/uploads/2021/03/Caracterisation-des-dechets-solides-au-Senegal-campagne-nationale.pdf> [accessed 28 July 2021].

UNDESA (2018) *World Urbanization Prospects: The 2018 Revision*, United Nations, New York.

UNEP/ISWA (2015) *Global Waste Management Outlook*, UN, New York <https://doi.org/10.18356/765baec0-en#>.

UN-Habitat (2009) *UN Demographic and Health Surveys, 2001-2003*, as cited in *State of the World's Cities 2008/2009*, Earthscan, London, p. 129.

UN-Habitat (2021) *Waste Wise Cities Tool – Step by Step Guide to Assess a City's MSWM Performance through SDG indicator 11.6.1 Monitoring* [pdf], UN-Habitat, Nairobi, <https://unhabitat.org/sites/default/files/2021-02/Waste%20wise%20cities%20tool%20-%20EN%207%20%281%29.pdf> [accessed 28 July 2021].

Velis, C. (2015) 'Circular economy and global secondary material supply chains', *Waste Management & Research* 33(5): 389–91 <https://doi.org/10.1177/0734242X15587641>.

Velis, C. (2017) 'Waste pickers in global south: informal recycling sector in a circular economy era', *Waste Management & Research* 35(4), 329–31.

Waste Concern (2016) *Bangladesh Waste Database 2014* [pdf], Waste Concern Technical Report Series, Dhaka, <http://wasteconcern.org/wp-content/uploads/2016/05/Waste-Data-Base_2014_Draft-Final.pdf> [accessed 28 July 2021].

Whiteman, A., Smith, P. and Wilson, D.C. (2001) 'Waste management: an indicator of urban governance', paper presented by DFID to UN-Habitat Global Conference on Urban Development, <http://davidcwilson.com/project/waste-management-an-indicator-of-urban-governance/> [accessed 28 July 2021].

Whiteman, A., Webster, M. and Wilson, D.C. (2021) 'The nine development bands: a conceptual framework and global theory for waste and development', *Waste Management and Research: The Journal for a Sustainable Circular Economy* 39(10): 1218-36 <https://doi.org/10.1177/0734242X211035926>.

WHO and UNICEF (2018) *JMP Methodology: 2017 Update and SDG Baselines* [pdf], United Nations Children's Fund and World Health Organization, New York, <https://washdata.org/report/jmp-methodology-2017-update> [accessed 28 July 2021].

Wiedinmyer, C., Yokelson, R.J. and Gullett, B.K. (2014) 'Global emissions of trace gases, particulate matter, and hazardous air pollutants from open burning of domestic waste, *Environmental Science and Technology* 48(16): 9523–30 <https://doi.org/10.1021/es502250z>.

WIEGO (2010) *Organizing Informal Waste Pickers: A Case Study of Bengaluru, India* [pdf], <http://www.wiego.org/sites/default/files/resources/files/Chengappa-Organizing-Informal-Waste-Pickers-India.pdf> [accessed 28 July 2021].

WIEGO (2014) *The Urban Informal Workforce: Waste Pickers / Recyclers Informal Economy Monitoring Study* [pdf], <https://www.wiego.org/sites/default/files/publications/files/IEMS-waste-picker-report.pdf> [accessed 28 July 2021].

WIEGO (2020) 'Réduction des déchets dans les villes côtières grâce au recyclage inclusif (ReWCC): étude de base sur les récupératrice.eur.s de la décharge de Mbeubeuss' [pdf], <https://www.wiego.org/sites/default/files/publications/file/Re%CC%81duction%20des%20de%CC%81chets%20-%20Rapport%20d%E2%80%99e%CC%81tude-version%20web.pdf> [accessed 28 July 2021].

Wijayanti, D.R. and Suryani, S. (2015) 'Waste bank as community-based environmental governance: a lesson learned from Surabaya', *Procedia – Social and Behavioral Sciences* 184: 171–9 <https://doi.org/10.1016/j.sbspro.2015.05.077>.

Wilson, D.C. (2007) 'Development drivers for waste management', *Waste Management & Research* 25(3): 198–207.

Wilson, D.C. (2021) 'The sustainable development goals as drivers of change', in Tudor, T. and Dutra, C.J.C (eds), *The Routledge Handbook of Waste, Resources and the Circular Economy*, Routledge, Abingdon.

Wilson, D.C., Velis, C. and Cheeseman. C., (2006) 'Role of the informal sector recycling in waste management in developing countries', *Habitat International*, 30: 797–808 <https://doi.org/10.1016/j.habitatint.2005.09.005>.

Wilson, D.C., Rodic, L., Cowing, M.J., Velis, C.A., Whiteman, A.D., Scheinberg, A., Vilches, R., Masterson, D., Stretz, J. and Oel, B. (2015) '"Wasteaware" benchmark indicators for integrated sustainable waste management in cities', Waste Management 35: 329–42 <https://doi.org/10.1016/j.wasman.2014.10.006>.

World Bank (2017) Senegal Municipal Solid Waste Management Project (P161477), Project Information Document/Integrated Safeguards Data Sheet [pdf], World Bank, Washington, DC, <https://documents1.worldbank.org/curated/en/581531500995135875/pdf/ITM00184-P161477-07-25-2017-1500995132357.pdf> [accessed 28 July 2021].

World Bank (2018a) Urban population growth (annual %) – Senegal [webpage], World Bank, Washington, DC, <https://data.worldbank.org/indicator/SP.URB.GROW?locations=SN> [accessed 1 August 2021].

World Bank (2018b) Population living in slums (% of urban population) [webpage], World Bank, Washington, DC, <https://data.worldbank.org/indicator/EN.POP.SLUM.UR.ZS?locations=SN> [accessed 1 August 2021].

WRA (2007) *The Impact of Pollution on Groundwater Resources* [pdf], Water Resources Authority Jamaica <https://www.nepa.gov.jm/LBS-Workshop/Impacts%20on%20Groundwater%20Resources%20-%20WRA.pdf> [accessed 1 August 2021].

www.ingramcontent.com/pod-product-compliance
Lightning Source LLC
Chambersburg PA
CBHW080902030426
42336CB00017B/2982